LAURE KIÉ & HARUNA KISHI

楽しい和ご

JAPANESE CUISINE

AN ILLUSTRATED

GUIDE

WRITTEN BY LAURE KIÉ
ILLUSTRATED BY HARUNA KISHI

FIREFLY BOOKS

CONTENTS

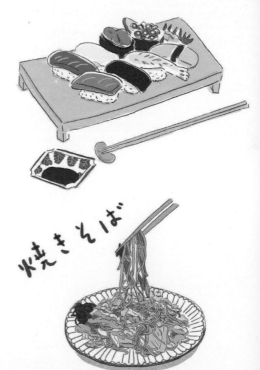

Other Signature Dishes...75

Cuisine by Theme..........93

Desserts and Beverages...113

Recipe Index...............126
Acknowledgements......127

日本料理

JAPANESE CUISINE

UNESCO has designated washoku (和食), Japanese culinary culture, as an Intangible Cultural Heritage of Humanity. Born of ancient traditions, Japanese cuisine is a real treasure that combines aesthetics, nutrition and flavors with an element unique to Japan: umami. This fifth taste (along with sweet, salty, sour and bitter), which could be translated as "deliciousness," gives dishes their depth.

けんちん汁

鰹節

針めもり

梨

THE FAMILY MEAL

家族でごはん

The Composition of a Meal

In Japanese, the word "rice" (gohan ご飯) also means "meal," indicating the importance of this grain as part of a Japanese meal. A typical meal is composed of a bowl of white rice, miso soup, vegetables, a protein (fish, meat or tofu), a small salad and condiments (usually pickled vegetables). A simple piece of fruit sometimes serves as dessert. Tea, beer or sake are served with dishes.

Okura (okra) with sesame sauce

Okara (soy pulp) with vegetables

Miso soup (see p. 23)

Simmered hijiki seaweed

Bowl of rice

Karaage (fried chicken) and raw vegetables

BREAKFAST
朝ごはん

Japanese omelet
(see p. 52)

Salted and
grilled salmon

Tsukemono
(see p. 24)

Grilled nori
seaweed

Rice

Miso
soup

In Japan, the traditional breakfast is savory. It is composed of miso soup and a bowl of rice served with condiments and nori seaweed. It can also include grilled fish! However, more and more families are now adopting a Western-style breakfast.

LUNCH
ごはん

Hiyayakko
tofu

Tsukemono
(see p. 24)

Miso
soup

Rice

Grilled fish
(see p. 80)

Soy sauce

KAISEKI SHOJIN RYORI

KAISEKI RYORI: QUINTESSENTIAL JAPANESE CUISINE

Whether it's the choice of ingredients based on the seasons, the balance of textures and colors, or the choice of serving dishes, this Japanese haute cuisine features a very codified ritual.

In kaiseki cuisine, pleasing the eyes is as important as pleasing the palate.

The meal is made up of a succession of small plates served in fine dishes. It must also include particular textures (crunchy, crispy, tender, sticky, etc.), cooking methods (grilled, simmered, raw, etc.) and flavors.

Kaiseki restaurant

Fall-inspired
kaiseki

懐石

8

SHOJIN RYORI: THE CUISINE OF THE TEMPLES

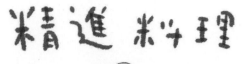

Food is extremely important in Zen. In Japanese Zen monasteries, the chef — the tenzo — is the second most important person. He oversees shojin ryori (the cuisine of Zen temples), which can be translated as "the cuisine that improves judgement." It contributes not only to a healthy body but also a healthy spirit!

The cuisine of Buddhist monasteries is, of course, completely vegetarian because taking a life is forbidden. But it is not confined to this single commandment. Other key principals of this cuisine that is closely connected to nature include preparing foods that are local, in season and in their natural state (non-processed) as well as avoiding waste.

Emblematic dishes of this cuisine include seasonal vegetable tempura, tofu-based dishes, simmered vegetables and the famous kenchin jiru soup.

Goma Dofu

This sesame tofu does not contain soy but is called "tofu" to evoke its texture. To make goma dofu, simply thicken a mixture of sesame puree, kuzu (starch) and water in a saucepan and let it cool in a mold.

Kenchin Jiru

This nutritious soup is made with a dashi broth of shiitake mushrooms along with kombu (see p. 22), root vegetables and tofu.

REGIONAL SPECIALTIES

日本の
特産品

Crab

Yudofu (tofu stew)/
Kyo-tsukemono (pickles)

Okonomiyaki
(see p. 96)

Yamaguchi

Fugu

Takoyaki
(see p. 97)

kyoto

hiroshima

Osaka

shikoku

Hobam
(grilled m
a magnolie

Hakata ramen
(see p. 65)/
Castella/Nori seaweed

Kyushu

Sanuki udon/
Yuzu/Katsuo
tataki
(see p. 81)

Okinawa

Goya (bitter cucumber)/
Champuru (meat and
vegetable stir-fry)

ombu
weed

ke

Uni-ikura don (rice with sea urchin and salmon roe)

hokkaido

Wanko soba

Tohoku

Imo-ni (potato stew)

Nigata

rice

Edo sushi/Monjayaki (variant of okonomiyaki)

Tokyo

Shizuoka

Unagi (grilled eel)/
Green tea/Wasabi

Because of its geography, Japan, which extends over 1,800 miles (3,000 km) from north to south, benefits from a broad range of climates, ranging from the harsh winter of Hokkaido to the tropical heat of the Okinawa islands. This offers up a wide variety of dishes.

お・皿　TABLEWARE

In Japan, there is a special emphasis on tableware because it contributes to the way of life and the full appreciation of a Japanese meal. Japanese ceramics is an ancient tradition, and all families have many artisan pieces.

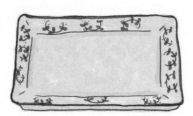

平ざら

Hirazara: rectangular plate
mainly for fish

椀

Wan: soup bowl with lid

茶椀

Chawan:
rice bowl

うどん鉢

Udon bachi:
udon bowl

丼ぶり
鉢

Donburi bachi:
donburi bowl

小鉢

Kobachi:
small bowl

Kyusu: teapot with side handle

醤油さし

Shoyu-sashi: soy sauce dispenser

急須

Dobin: teapot with arch handle

湯のみ

Yunomi: teacup

蕎麦猪口

Soba choko: small dish for soba sauce

箸置き

Hashioki: chopstick rest

お鍋

Donabe: clay pot

UTENSILS & CHOPSTICKS

In Japan, utensils are quite different from the ones we have in our kitchens. With these few details, you will better understand them.

卵焼き器

Tamagoyaki pan:
rectangular pan
for making Japanese
omelets
(see p. 52)

お金鍋

Yukihira nabe:
hammered saucepan
and its wooden lid
(otoshi buta)

寿司セット

Suribachi:
ceramic mortar
with grooves and
wooden pestle

おろし金

Oroshigane:
grater without
holes for daikon, ginger
and garlic

鮫皮おろし

Wasabi oroshi:
sharkskin
wasabi grater

菜箸

Ryoribashi:
wooden cooking
chopsticks (longer than
those used for eating)

ざる

Zaru:
bamboo sieve

すり鉢

Sushi oke:
wooden plate for making
sushi rice with vinegar
(see p. 33) with the help
of a shamoji (spatula).
The makisu is the bamboo
mat for rolling maki
(see p. 40)

Hocho: Japanese Knives

These are essential tools in a Japanese kitchen because each food item needs to be carefully cut so it can be eaten with chopsticks. The quality of the steel used and the know-how of the knife makers — passed down from generation to generation by bladesmiths since the time of the samurai — produce exceptionally sharp blades.

包丁

Deba: typical beveled knife

出刃

Nakiri: rectangular knife used for slicing and chopping

菜切り

Gyuto: chef's knife

牛刃

Santoku: multipurpose knife

三徳

Yanagiba: long sashimi knife

柳刃

Ohashi: Chopsticks

How to use them

1 Place one chopstick on the end of your ring finger and in the crease between your thumb and index finger. This chopstick will remain fixed.

2 Take the second chopstick between the top of your thumb, index and middle finger. Always keep the tips of the two chopsticks at the same height.

3 The second chopstick is the one that moves.

What Not to Do with Your Chopsticks

- Stick chopsticks in a bowl of rice
- Stab food with chopsticks
- Move dishes using chopsticks
- Point your chopsticks at someone
- Use your personal chopsticks to take food from a serving dish

PREPARED FOODS

柱料

Before diving into Japanese cuisine, it is important to familiarize yourself with its ingredients. Thanks to cooks' growing interest in Japanese food, many large grocery stores carry Japanese ingredients, and there are also numerous online sources.

お酢

Rice vinegar

みりん

Mirin: sweet rice wine

お酒

Sake: rice-derived alcohol

だしパック

Dashi: dissolvable bouillon powder for making soups and stews

味噌

Miso: fermented soy paste, with rice or barley

蒟蒻

Konnyaku: a starchy block of the root vegetable konjac

鰹節

Katsuobushi: dried bonito flakes, mainly used as a base for dashi broth

豆腐

Tofu: soy "cheese" made from curdled soy milk (see p. 83)

梅干し

Umeboshi: Japanese pickled plums with purple shiso leaves

パン粉

Panko: Japanese bread crumbs (see p. 78)

天ぷら粉

Tempura flour: makes very light fritters (see p. 76)

マヨネーズ

Kewpie mayonnaise

とんかつ ソース

Tonkatsu sauce: used for breaded pork and croquettes (see p. 79)

焼そば ソース

Yakisoba sauce: used in stir-fried noodles (see p. 71)

お好み焼き ソース

Okonomiyaki sauce: used on savory pancakes (see p. 96)

やきとりの たれ

Yakitori sauce: used on skewers (see p. 95)

お醤油

Soy sauce

ぽん酢

Ponzu sauce: seasoning made from Japanese citrus fruits (yuzu, sudachi) and soy sauce

FRUITS, VEGETABLES AND SEAWEED

日本の野菜

大根

Daikon: This white radish is Japanese cuisine's most representative vegetable. It's used raw in salads, grated and marinated to make a condiment, and cooked in simmered dishes.

山葵

Wasabi: A root found in mountains that is similar to horseradish. Once grated, this green root produces a paste that is served with sushi.

椎茸

Mushrooms: Mushrooms are omnipresent in Japanese cuisine. Shiitake (above), shimeji and enoki are cooked in stews, tempura and soups.

蓮根

Renkon (lotus root): This root vegetable has distinctive holes that look like alveoli. It is fried, stewed, lightly fried and even pickled.

茗荷

Myoga: This plant from the ginger family is used like a shallot. It is often used to garnish salads or cold noodle dishes in the summer.

南瓜

Kabocha: This Japanese winter squash has a tender flesh with notes of chestnut. It is simmered (see p. 109) or made into tempura (see p. 77).

Shiso: This aromatic herb from the mint family, also called "perilla," often accompanies a sushi platter.

Goya: This bitter and rough cucumber is the speciality of Okinawa. It is reputed to be rich in nutrients.

Mitsuba: This very aromatic Japanese parsley is mostly used in soups.

Kombu: Seaweed used as the base for dashi broth.

Wakame: Seaweed used in soups and salads.

Nori: Seaweed that has been pressed into sheets.

Yuzu: This delicately flavored yellow citrus fruit is common in Japanese cuisine, particularly in ponzu sauce and desserts.

Nashi: Juicy and crunchy Japanese pear.

Kaki: This orange-colored fruit can be eaten raw or dried.

ORDERING AT A RESTAURANT

Irrashaimase! (Welcome!) That is how guests are received when they enter a Japanese restaurant. But before lifting the noren, the facade of a traditional restaurant can be a bit disconcerting because you can't see what's inside and menus are not always posted.

The Restaurant's Facade

The noren is the curtain that hangs in front of the entrance of a restaurant (as well as a store or house). The restaurant's name and logo are printed on the noren.

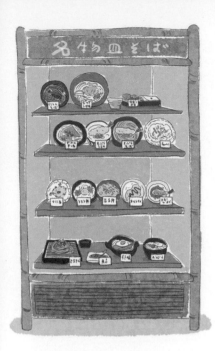

Displays

Display cases with dishes can been seen in front of many restaurants in Japan. These plastic samples look like real dishes and can help you choose your meal!

ショーケース

御献立

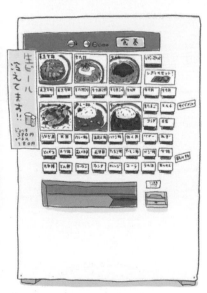

券売機

Vending Machines

In some popular restaurants, you can order and pay for your meal at a vending machine before entering the restaurant. There are often photos on each button, which makes ordering easy. The vending machines dispense a ticket, which you present upon entering the restaurant.

Signage

In restaurants, you may not always be brought a menu, as they are sometimes hung on the wall. "Omakase" is a term that means "I'll leave it up to you." It indicates you wish to let the chef decide on the course of the meal. This is common in Japan, and an excellent way to discover new flavors!

出汁 DASHI BROTH

Dashi broth is the essential base in Japanese cuisine. It is used for making many dishes, like miso soup and stews, but it is also used in sauces and to cook vegetables, fish and meat. There is ready-to-use dashi powder, but it is simple to make it yourself with dried kombu, katsuobushi, shiitake mushrooms or even iriko (also called niboshi), which are small, dried sardines.

Kombu Katsuobushi Dried shiitake mushrooms Iriko

Preparation

Heat a piece of kombu, about 4 in. (10 cm) long, in 4 cups (1 L) water. Just before stock begins to boil, remove from the heat and add ¾ oz. (20 g), or about 1½ to 2 cups, katsuobushi. Let it settle to the bottom of the pot and then strain.

Tip
To make dashi with shiitake or iriko, let them soak in the water for 2 hours before adding the kombu and heating the mixture.

SUIMONO

吸い物

This is a clear soup (i.e., without miso, which clouds the broth) with a subtle flavor. It is important to use quality ingredients to enjoy the full flavor of this broth.

SERVES 4

1 Bring 4 cups (1 L) dashi broth to a boil with 1 tbsp. (15 ml) white soy sauce, 1 tbsp. (15 ml) mirin and ½ tsp. (2 ml) salt.

2 In the center of each bowl, place 1 peeled cooked shrimp, 1 sprig of chopped mitsuba and a little yuzu zest.

3 Pour the broth on top.

MISO SOUP

Miso soup is part of almost all Japanese meals, served with a bowl of rice. There are many ways to prepare it, and a good number of seasonal vegetables can be added to it. The vegetables are cooked in the dashi broth before incorporating the miso paste, which should not be brought to a boil.

みそ汁

SERVES 4

1 Bring 6 oz. (160 g) diced silken tofu and 4 cups (1 L) dashi broth (see opposite) to a boil.

2 Remove a small ladle of broth from the saucepan, mix with about 3½ tbsp. (50 ml) miso of your choice (different types of miso can be more or less salty; taste your soup and add a little more if needed), and then incorporate it into the mixture.

3 Add 2¾ oz. (80 g) wakame, rehydrated. Remove from heat just before it boils. Split the soup among 4 bowls.

豆腐

Tofu

出汁

Dashi

味噌

Miso

わかめ

Wakame

SAUCES AND CONDIMENTS
ソース

TAKUAN

沢庵

MAKES 1 LARGE JAR

1. Peel and slice 1 daikon. Combine with 1 tbsp. (15 ml) salt in a bowl. Let stand for 2 hours.

2. Bring ⅔ cup (150 ml) rice vinegar, ⅔ cup (150 ml) water, ¼ cup (60 ml) sugar and 1 pinch of turmeric powder (for color) to a boil in a saucepan and cook for 2 minutes.

3. Pour the contents over the daikon. Put in a jar and refrigerate for 2 days before eating.

Tip
Ideally served with white rice.

漬け物

CABBAGE TSUKEMONO

1. Slice ½ napa cabbage (Chinese cabbage).

2. Place the cabbage with 1 tbsp. (15 ml) salt and 1 piece of dried kombu sliced into thin strips into a freezer bag. Mix well, seal the bag and let stand in the refrigerator for at least 4 hours.

3. Squeeze the cabbage with your hands to remove the maximum amount of liquid before eating.

Tip
Ideally served with white rice.

FURIKAKE

MAKES ABOUT ⅓ CUP (75 ML) OF FURIKAKE

ふりかけ

1 Combine ⅓ cup (75 ml) sesame seeds, ½ tsp. (2 ml) sesame oil, 1 tsp. (5 ml) sugar and 2 tsp. (10 ml) salt in a bowl.

2 Spread this mixture on a baking sheet lined with parchment paper. Bake at 350°F (180°C) for 12 minutes.

3 Blend the mixture in a food processor with 1 sheet of roughly torn nori.

Tip
Ideal for sprinkling on white rice.

てりやきソース

TERIYAKI SAUCE

MAKES 1¼ CUPS (300 ML) OF SAUCE

1 Bring ⅔ cup (150 ml) soy sauce, ½ cup (125 ml) sake, ½ cup (125 ml) mirin and ¼ cup (60 ml) sugar to a boil in a saucepan.

2 Reduce for 5 minutes, stirring occasionally.

Tip
Ideally served on fish (see p. 54).

GOMADARE SAUCE

MAKES 1 CUP (250 ML) OF SAUCE

ごまだれ

1 Dissolve ½ cup (125 ml) sesame paste a little at a time in ½ cup (125 ml) dashi broth (see p. 22), stirring constantly.

2 Incorporate 1 grated garlic clove, 1 tsp. (5 ml) salt, 1 tbsp. (15 ml) mirin, 1 tbsp. (15 ml) rice vinegar and 2 tbsp. (30 ml) soy sauce until the sauce becomes smooth.

Tip
Ideally served on vegetables.

CUTTING TECHNIQUES FOR FRUITS AND VEGETABLES

野菜の切り方

Cutting is of utmost importance in Japanese cuisine, not only for presentation but also because it influences cooking and texture.

斜め切り

Diagonal cut (nanamegiri): This is a common cut that creates a more aesthetically pleasing shape and a larger surface area than a simple slice into rounds. It is mainly used for leeks, cucumbers and carrots.

乱切り

Rotational cut (rangiri): This diagonal cut involves turning the vegetable slightly after each slice. This irregular cut is mainly used for vegetables to be simmered because cooking is more even.

Paper-thin sheet (katsuramuki) and then thin julienne cut (hosogiri): A large section of daikon is continuously peeled with a knife to obtain a thin sheet in one piece. The sheet is then cut into equally sized rectangles that are stacked on top of each other and finally cut into a very thin julienne.

細切り

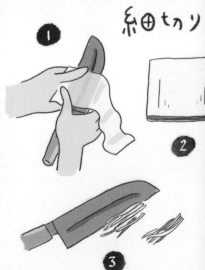

さきがき

Shaving (sasagaki): This cut involves shaving vegetables with a knife, as you would to sharpen a pencil or stick. This technique is used particularly for gobo (burdock root).

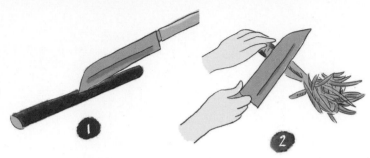

面取り

Rounded cut (mentori): Cubes of vegetables are rounded on all sides. This technique avoids damaging root vegetables or squash, like kabocha, when cooking.

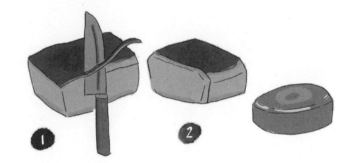

ねじり梅

Plum blossom cut (nejiri ume): This cut is mainly used for carrots, which give a splash of color to simmered dishes. Cut the carrots into thick, round slices and then use a shape cutter on each slice. With a knife, make a "v" shape incision between the petals.

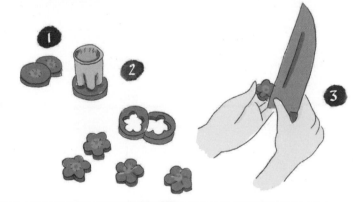

うさぎりんご

Rabbit cut (usagi ringo): This technique is used for apples. Cut the apple in 8 pieces. Remove the core and seeds. With a knife, cut a "v" in the skin and then peel the skin back to the base of the V. Lift up the skin in the V shape.

ごはん類

ALL ABOUT RICE

In Japanese, the word for "rice" (gohan ご飯) also means "meal." Rice is the central element of Japanese cuisine. All the richness and subtlety of Japanese cuisine is in the art of how dishes are prepared and what they're paired with. In that regard, the Japanese are full of imagination and creativity. While a multitude of rice recipes exist, there are still some basics to know, both in terms of cooking methods and varieties, to get the best out of this magical grain, which is the most consumed grain in the world.

THE DiFFERENT RiCE DiSHES

From classic sushi to mochi, Japanese cuisine offers a wide variety of rice dishes. Here are some staples that are often found on Japanese tables.

Temaki

Literally, "temaki" means "hand rolled". To make temaki, you don't need a bamboo mat, just your hands! See recipe on p. 40.

Maki

Maki, which means "roll" in Japanese, is a type of sushi roll wrapped in a sheet of nori. The only hard part is to master the movement described on p. 40!

Chirashi Sushi

These bowls of vinegared rice with toppings (vegetables, eggs, fish) can be defined as "scattered" sushi. It's a very easy dish to make (see recipe on p. 39).

Nigiri

Nigiri is quite similar to sashimi. While sashimi is generally prepared raw fish, with nigiri, a ball of rice is generally topped with raw fish. Learn how to shape nigiri on p. 38.

炊きこみご飯

Takikomi

Rice is cooked together with vegetables, seasoning and possibly fish or chicken. This cooking method delicately flavors the rice.

Onigiri

Onigiri is a healthy and portable Japanese-style sandwich. It consists of a (often triangular) ball of rice with a filling. See p. 46.

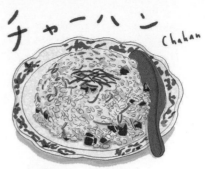

Chahan

This wok-fried rice dish originally comes from China. It's great for using up leftover rice!

Ochazuke

This dish, which means "with tea," is a hit in Japan for its delicate flavor. You simply pour tea on cooked rice, and it is often served with plum umeboshi (pickled plum) and seaweed.

Mochi Isobe Maki

Made with steamed sticky rice that is pounded, mochi is mainly eaten around the new year. It is often eaten as isobe maki, meaning it is grilled and wrapped in a sheet of nori and then seasoned simply with soy sauce.

Donburi

This is a popular dish that consists of a bowl of rice topped with a number of ingredients (tempura, tonkatsu, curry, etc.). See the recipe for oyakodon on p. 44 and gyudon on p. 45.

JAPANESE RICE

ご飯の炊き方

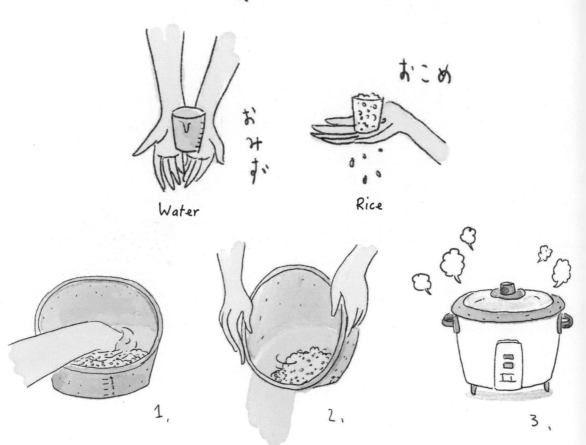

おみず

Water

おこめ

Rice

1,

2,

3,

Cooking Rice

For quantities, the rule is to use equal parts rice and water. For example, for 4 large bowls, you will need 3 cups (750 ml) Japanese rice and 3 cups (750 ml) water.

1 Rinse the rice until the water runs clear.

2 Drain it and put it in the rice cooker with water.

3 Cook according to your appliance's directions and let it rest for at least 10 minutes.

Trick: If you don't have a rice cooker, don't worry! Combine the rice and water in a saucepan, cover, bring to a boil and cook for 12 minutes on very low heat. Remove the saucepan from the heat and let the rice rest for about 10 minutes, covered.

すし飯

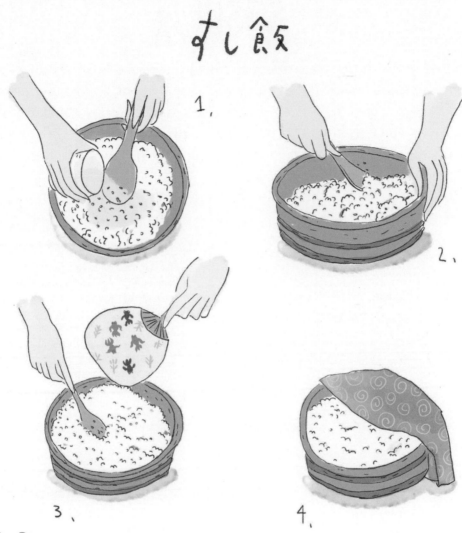

1.

2.

3.

4.

Sushi Rice

1 Pour cooked rice that's still warm in a deep dish and sprinkle sushi rice vinegar* overtop (2 cups [500 ml] for the amount of rice on the opposite page).

2 Gently combine the rice and vinegar using a rice spoon (or a flat spatula), so as not to crush the grains.

3 Once the rice is fully coated with vinegar, cool it with a hand fan: It will give the rice a beautiful, glistening appearance.

4 Let the rice rest under a damp cloth until ready to serve so it doesn't dry out.

*Tip: You can easily prepare your sushi vinegar by dissolving 3 tbsp. (45 ml) sugar and 1 tsp. (5 ml) salt in 2 cups (500 ml) rice vinegar.

SUSHI

Sushi is made from vinegared rice and toppings. While vinegared rice, the base, is always used, sushi's shape can vary significantly. The most common shape in Japan is nigiri sushi, but there are many other presentations: maki (the rolls popular in North America), temaki (hand rolls), chirashi (bowl of vinegared rice with toppings), temari (balls) and oshi sushi (pressed), among others.

Traditional Sushi-ya

寿司屋

In Japan, there are numerous places to eat sushi. You can choose a traditional sushi-ya (sushi restaurant), where customers sit at the counter and the chefs face them, making sushi to order in a cozy atmosphere. The high-quality fish and shellfish are displayed behind glass at the counter.

The color of the plate indicates the price of the sushi.

Kaiten Sushi-ya (Revolving Sushi)

Sushi travels on a conveyor belt.

回転寿司や

In a completely different atmosphere, a kaiten sushi-ya is a restaurant where the sushi is presented on small plates and passes in front of customers on a conveyor belt. Diners just need to reach out and pick the dish that speaks to them. It's a fun way to eat sushi!

TYPES OF SUSHI
寿司ネタ

マグロ

Maguro: *tuna*

穴子

Anago: *sea eel*

サーモン

Salmon

玉子

Tamago: *egg*

アジ

Aji: *horse mackerel*

いくら

Ikura: *salmon roe*

タコ

Tako: *octopus*

えび

Ebi: *shrimp*

ウニ

Uni: *sea urchin*

CUTTING FISH

THE DIFFERENT PARTS OF A TUNA

Tuna is the king of raw fish. However, depending on the quality of the pieces, its flavor and texture can vary greatly... and its cost can vary too!

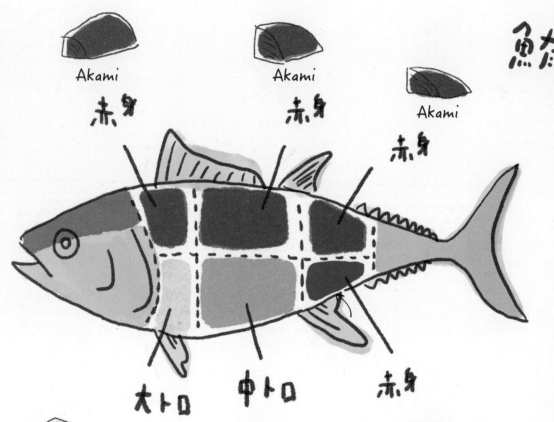

Akami

赤身

Akami

赤身

Akami

赤身

鮪

大トロ

中トロ

赤身

O-toro:
the best part;
extra fatty with a
tender, pinkish flesh

Chu-toro:
fatty part of the
tuna; it has light
red flesh

Akami:
the most
commonly found
part; it has bright
red flesh

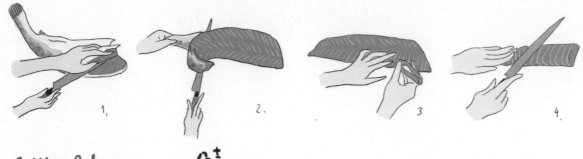

Cutting Salmon 鮭

1 Slice open the first fillet of the scaled salmon, going from the head toward the tail, following the spine. Pull back the fillet, taking care to always have the knife's blade as close as possible to the bones, to keep the flesh intact. Remove the spine in the same way to obtain the second fillet.

2 Using a sashimi knife, remove the skin from each fillet. Use the knife to also remove all the gray parts close to the skin and the hard white parts. Keep these pieces, along with the head and bones, to flavor soups or broths — for example, you can add them to miso soup (p. 23).

3 With a tweezer, remove any small bones while holding the flesh with two fingers.

4 Cut the fillets into slices of the desired size, depending on use (sashimi, maki, chirashi, etc.).

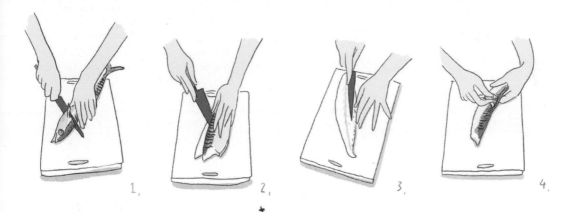

Cutting Mackerel 鯖

1 Cut the head off. Slice the belly of the fish to remove the guts (be sure to remove the blood found at the bottom of the belly by scratching this area with your thumb). Rinse thoroughly with water.

2 Remove the first fillet in the same way as with the salmon, described. Turn the fish over and cut out the second fillet.

3 Remove all the hard parts around the edge of the fillets along with the bones.

4 Remove the skin with the tip of the knife's blade (the thin skin can be removed by hand). Cut fillets into slices of the desired size, depending on use.

SHAPING SUSHI

握り寿司のにぎり方

Shaping sushi is practically an art in Japan: It takes about 10 years of apprenticeship to become a sushi master! But, rest assured, you can still enjoy sushi by following the advice of our chef, Ito-san!

1 

1   Wet your hand and take a small amount of vinegared rice (see p. 33) in the palm of your hand. Lightly press the rice by rolling it to create an oval ball.

2 

2   With your finger, put a dab of wasabi at the center of the fish.

3 

3   Place the fish on the rice. With two fingers, press down on the fish so it sticks to the rice.

4   Place the shaped nigiri sushi on a serving plate. It's ready!

4 

できあがり

CHIRASHI SUSHI ちらし ずし

SERVES 2

たまご
Egg

いくら
Salmon roe

蓮根
Lotus root

さやいんげん

椎茸

Flat beans

Shiitake
mushrooms

1 Bring 2 dried shiitake mushrooms to a boil in a small saucepan of water. Remove from heat and let infuse for 30 minutes (keep the cooking water). After removing the stems, chop the mushrooms. Remove the ends from 4 green beans and slice the beans. Peel and slice 1½ in. (4 cm) lotus root (or daikon or long radish) into rounds.

2 Cook the vegetables in a pot with ½ cup (125 ml) water , 3 tbsp. (45 ml) soy sauce and 3 tbsp. (45 ml) mirin, until the ingredients have absorbed all the liquid.

3 Beat 1 egg with 1 pinch of salt. Add half to an oiled pan to make a thin omelet. Cook for 1 minute, and then turn it over and cook for a few seconds more. Place the omelet on a board and repeat with the rest of the beaten egg. Stack the two omelets, roll them up and thinly slice.

4 Split the eggs, cooked vegetables, salmon roe and strips of nori between 2 big bowls of vinegared rice (see p. 33).

巻きずし MAKI & TEMAKI

Making Maki

1 Place a sheet of nori on a maki mat. Spread a layer of rice on three-quarters of the nori.

2 Arrange the filling in lines on the rice.

3 While holding the filling with your fingers, lift the edge of the mat closest to you and fold it over the filling. Press the mat with your hands to form a cylinder. With one hand, roll up the maki little by little, while pulling the mat with your other hand. With each roll, gently press the maki.

4 Remove the mat and cut the roll in 8 or 10 bite-sized pieces.

Temaki

This is my favorite dish for when I invite friends over. I arrange all of the ingredients on the table, so that everyone prepares their own temaki throughout the meal. It's very social and a sure hit!

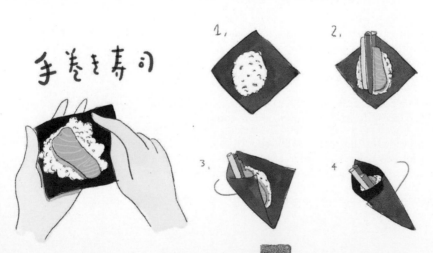

To make temaki, take a sheet of nori that's been cut into 4 pieces, place 1 tbsp. (15 ml) sushi rice (see p. 33) in the center, then add the fillings and fold into a cone. Dip in soy sauce and enjoy.

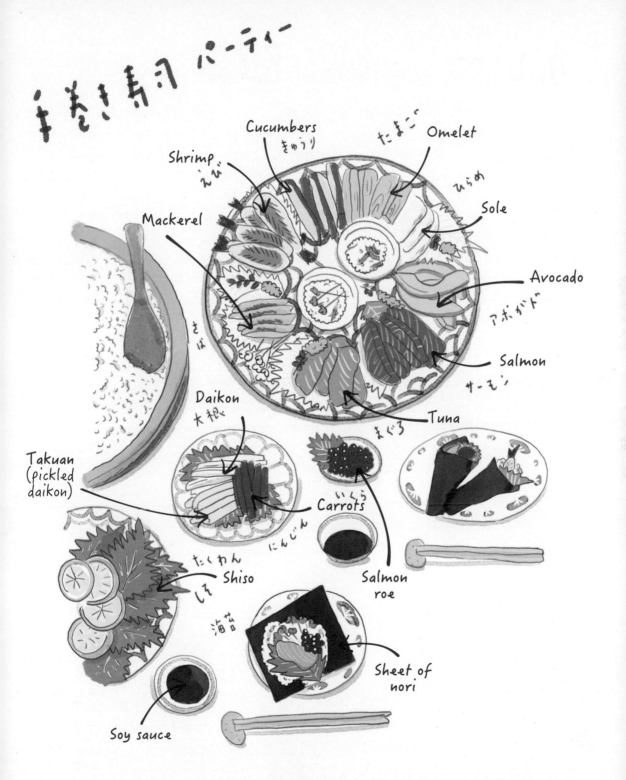

カレー KARE RICE

"Kare" is the Japanese word for "curry." It is a very popular dish in Japan and is generally served with rice, but it can also be eaten with udon noodles. Japanese curry is sold in cubes, similar to bouillon, and is prepared by stirring into a liquid. It's very easy to make, and the perfect family dish!

SERVES 4

1 Heat a little sunflower oil in a saucepan, and then cook 1 minced garlic clove, 1 tsp. (5 ml) minced fresh ginger, 2 chopped carrots and ½ onion for 3 to 4 minutes on high heat, stirring regularly.

2 Add 2 boneless chicken thighs, cubed, and brown for 2 to 3 minutes, stirring constantly. Add 8 button mushrooms cut into quarters and cook, stirring, for 2 to 3 minutes.

3 Add 2½ cups (625 ml) water and let everything cook for 15 minutes over low heat.

4 Stir in ½ grated apple and 3 oz. (80 g) Japanese curry. Simmer for 5 minutes over low heat, stirring constantly to dissolve the curry and thicken the sauce.

5 Divide the kare among 4 bowls of hot rice (see p. 32) and serve immediately. If desired, add toppings (see below).

Kare Toppings

Japanese curry is always served with toppings. It could be a simple hard-boiled egg or small condiments, such as fukujinzuke (sweet vegetable pickles) or rakkyo (small pickled onions).

たまご Hard-boiled egg

Rakkyo

らっきょう

Fukujinzuke

福神漬け

42

Water
お水

Chicken
鶏肉

Garlic
にんにく

Kare
(curry)
カレーのルウ

Apple
りんご

Ginger
生姜

Mushrooms
きのこ

Onions
玉葱

Carrots
人参

DONBURI

OYAKODON

SERVES 4

1 Bring ¾ cup (175 ml) dashi broth to a boil and add 1 large diced boneless chicken thigh, 1 thinly sliced onion, and some soy sauce and mirin. Cook for about 5 minutes over medium heat.

2 Combine 4 eggs in a bowl without beating them.

3 Pour the eggs into the pan while gently stirring. Cook until the eggs set.

4 Divide the cooked rice among 4 bowls. Add the mixture on top, and then garnish with mitsuba, green onion tops and strips of nori.

Eggs Mirin Soy sauce Chicken Onions

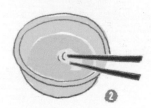

Mitsuba

Green onions

Nori

親子丼

Oyakodon

44

GYUDON

SERVES 4

gyu don
牛丼

Water
みず

Soy sauce
醤油

Beef slices
牛肉スライス

Onion
玉ねぎ

Mirin
みりん

Sake
酒

Sugar
さとう

1 Bring ¼ cup (60 ml) soy sauce, ¼ cup (60 ml) mirin, ¼ cup (60 ml) sake, ¼ cup (60 ml) water and 1 tbsp. (15 ml) sugar to a boil.

2 Add 1 thinly sliced onion, cover and cook for 5 minutes, and then add ¾ lb. (320 g) very thin slices of beef. Continue cooking until almost no liquid remains.

3 Divide the mixture among 4 bowls of hot cooked rice (see p. 32). Garnish with pickled ginger before serving.

おにぎり ONIGIRI

The Different Shapes

Onigiri are snacks that Japanese people eat at any time of the day. These portable rice sandwiches are a practical way to use up leftover rice.

Cylindrical:
This shape is found in bento boxes.

Rounded:
This shape is simple to make with plastic wrap.

Triangular:
This shape is the most common and definitely the easiest to eat.

Sandwich (onigirazu):
Somewhere between an onigiri and a sandwich, this new shape emerged just a few years ago.

Other kawaii shapes:
Onigiri can be made into an endless number of shapes. These edible animal and flower shapes are intended for children.

おにぎりの 握り方

Shaping Onigiri

1 Wet and lightly salt your hands.

2 Take a good amount of rice with a wooden spatula.

3 Place the filling in the middle of the rice.

4 Gently compact the rice to form a triangle.

5 The trick is to turn the triangle between your hands to apply even pressure on all three sides, without compressing the rice, which must not be crushed.

6 Once shaped, wrap a strip of nori around the onigiri.

ONIGIRI FLAVORS AND FILLINGS

While umeboshi plum and nori are the two most common ingredients, there are infinite possibilities for onigiri!

おにぎり

梅干し おにぎり

Classic:
1. umeboshi (pickled plum)
2. nori

しそゆかり おにぎり

Fragrant:
1. yukari (purple shiso salt)
2. green shiso leaf

鮭とごま塩 おにぎり

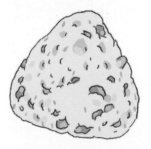

Salmon:
1. cooked, salted and
flaked salmon
2. gomashio (a mixture
of sesame seeds and salt)

炒り卵とえんどう豆 おにぎり

Soft:
1. scrambled eggs
2. cooked peas

Onigiri
おにぎり

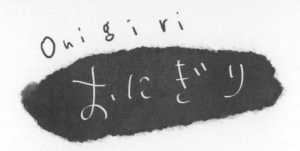

Trick: You can also use an onigiri mold to form the triangles.

卵巻きふりかけおにぎり

Traditional:
1. thin egg omelet (see p. 39)
2. furikake (see p. 25)

ツナマヨおにぎり

Tuna and mayo:
1. flaked canned tuna
2. mayonnaise
3. nori

焼き味噌おにぎり

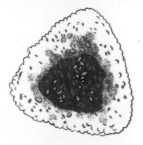

Grilled with miso:
1. miso
2. toasted sesame oil
3. chives
Place the onigiri under the broiler for a few minutes.

えび天おにぎり

Shrimp tempura:
1. shrimp tempura (see p. 77)
2. nori

BENTO

Bento is an institution in Japan. From an early age, children bring their lunch to school, lovingly prepared by their mother and stored in a pretty, compartmentalized box called a "bento." These meal boxes are also commonly brought to offices and picnics by adults.

Accessories

They are equally decorative and practical. Here are some accessories to complete your bento!

おべんとう

Paper wrappers and silicone molds:
separate the bento into compartments

Separators:
prevent foods from mixing

Picks:
used to garnish and to help make the contents easier to eat

Sauce containers:
hold liquid sauces

Condiment containers:
hold solid seasonings

Shape cutters:
used to cut bread and vegetables

Arranging Your Bento

1 Place the rice first, and then add a lettuce leaf or an aromatic on one side of the rice to separate it from the rest of the contents.

2 Place the main components, taking care to arrange everything nicely.

3 Fill in empty spaces with vegetables or sauce containers that can easily squeeze in.

4 Lastly, garnish the bento by decorating it with picks, condiments sprinkled on the rice or carved vegetables. It's now ready!

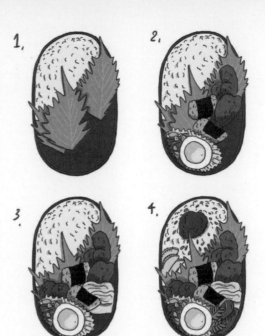

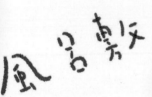

Furoshiki: Wrapping Your Bento

Furoshiki is a square fabric used to wrap different objects to take with you or offer as a gift. There are many techniques to beautifully wrap your bento. Here are two examples.

A rectangular bento:

A circular bento:

BENTO FOODS

Step-by-Step Tamagoyaki

Tamagoyaki is a Japanese omelet that has the distinction of being cooked in several layers. It can be found in most bento boxes.

だし巻き卵

MAKES 1 OMELET

1 Beat 4 eggs together with ¼ cup (60 ml) dashi broth and 1 pinch of salt in a bowl.

2 Heat a little oil in a tamagoyaki pan, and then pour a small amount of the beaten eggs to form a thin omelet.

3 Roll the omelet to one side of the pan.

4 Pour another small amount of the beaten eggs. Gently lift the previously rolled omelet to allow some egg to flow underneath. Let it set, and then roll the new omelet to the opposite side of the pan.

5 Continue until all the beaten egg is used up. Using a spatula, lightly brown the omelette on all sides.

6 Slice the omelet and add to the bento.

Toppings

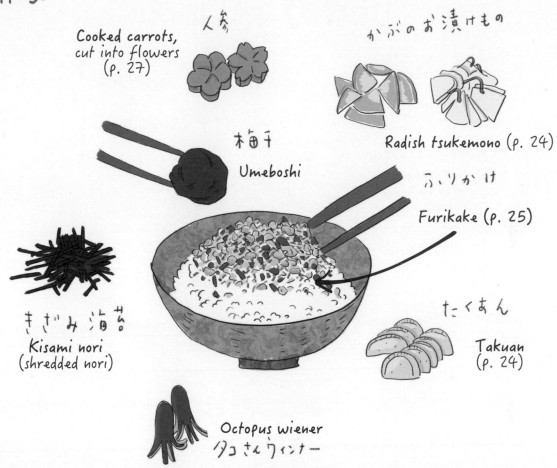

Cooked carrots, cut into flowers (p. 27)

人参

かぶのお漬けもの

Radish tsukemono (p. 24)

梅干

Umeboshi

ふりかけ

Furikake (p. 25)

きざみ海苔

Kisami nori (shredded nori)

たくあん

Takuan (p. 24)

Octopus wiener
タコさんウィンナー

Octopus Wiener

How to cut a wiener in the shape of an octopus

1 Cut the wiener diagonally in half.

2 Cut the bottom half of each half-wiener to create tentacles.

3 Boil the octopus wiener for 1 minute to give the tentacles a nice shape.

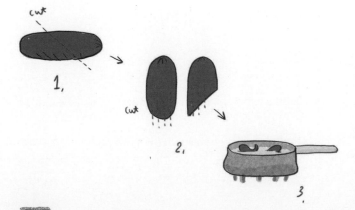

BENTO RECIPES

BENTO TERIYAKI

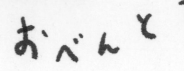

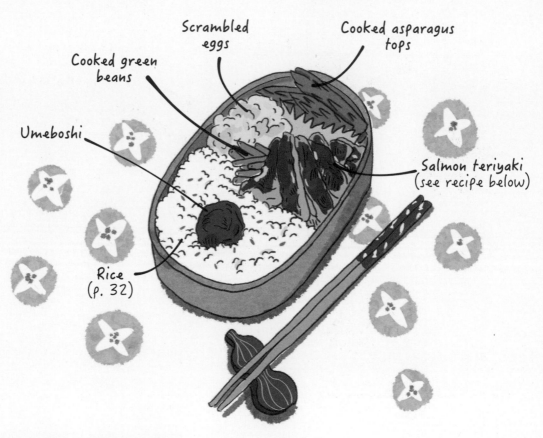

Scrambled eggs

Cooked asparagus tops

Cooked green beans

Umeboshi

Salmon teriyaki (see recipe below)

Rice (p. 32)

SALMON TERIYAKI

SERVES 2

1 Remove the skin and bones from ½ lb. (200 g) salmon fillets.

2 Combine 2 tbsp. (30 ml) soy sauce, 2 tbsp. (30 ml) mirin, 1 tbsp. (15 ml) sake and 3 tbsp. (45 ml) sugar in a bowl.

3 Cook the salmon in a pan on medium heat for 1 to 2 minutes on each side, depending on the thickness.

4 Pour the contents of the bowl into the pan, coat the salmon in sauce and reduce for 30 seconds.

KAWAII* BENTO

KAWAii
おべんとう

Tamagoyaki
(see p. 52)

Rolled ham &
asparagus

Bear onigiri
(see below)

Cooked
broccoli

Nori

Umeboshi

*Kawaii (かわいい) means
"cute" in Japanese.

BEAR ONIGIRI

SERVES 1

1. In a big bowl, combine 1 bowl of cooked rice (see p. 32) with 1 pinch of salt and ½ tsp. (2 ml) sesame seeds.

2. Using plastic wrap, make 1 large, slightly oval ball of rice for the head and 2 small balls for the ears. Assemble the ears and the head.

3. Make the eyes with nori, the cheeks with slices of carrot, the muzzle with umeboshi or a round slice of mozzarella topped with a pea and a strip of nori for the mouth.

ALL ABOUT NOODLES

Noodles (麺, men), like rice, are a staple in Japanese cuisine. Noodles, which can be eaten at any time of the day, are prepared in a number of ways, including in broth, cold, simmered in a stew, fried in a wok, in salads and in pot stickers. There are many small restaurants where you can stop in for a quick bowl of delicious noodles served in a broth that has simmered for hours. And in Japan, it is acceptable to make noise when eating noodles, so don't be shy — slurp them!

NOODLE VARIETIES

There are a wide variety of noodles in Japan, with traditional noodles like soba, udon or somen on one hand and Chinese-inspired noodles like ramen and yakisoba on the other.

Soba

"Soba" means "buckwheat" in Japanese. These noodles are the symbol of a refined and healthy cuisine. They are prepared very simply — hot in soup or cold with tsuyu sauce (see p. 67).

Ramen

These wheat noodles, originally from China, were introduced to Japan at the start of the 20th century. Served in a broth with a soy sauce or miso base, they have experienced a real boom with the advent of instant noodles. However, there's nothing like eating a good bowl at a ramen restaurant or a recipe you've made yourself (see p. 62)!

Udon

Along with soba and ramen, these are the most consumed noodles in Japan. Made from wheat flour, salt and water, udon noodles are white and vary in size, depending on the region. Dried or fresh (vacuum packed), they are served in broth, with toppings or as a cold dish.

Somen

These very thin white noodles are made from wheat flour. They are eaten cold during the summer and seasoned with tsuyu sauce.

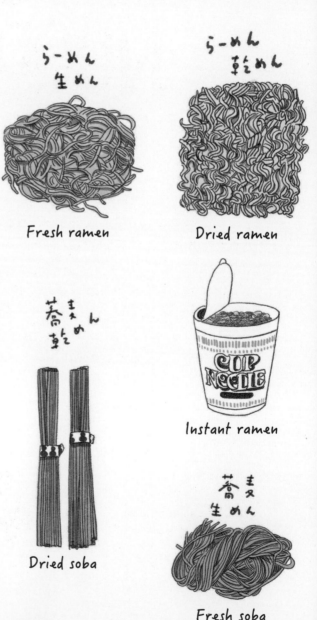

らーめん
生めん

Fresh ramen

らーめん
乾めん

Dried ramen

蕎麦
乾めん

Dried soba

Instant ramen

蕎麦
生めん

Fresh soba

麺
Noodles

そうめん

Dried udon

素麺

Somen

焼きそば
めん

Yakisoba

茶蕎麦

Cha soba
(green tea soba)

うどん
めん

Fresh udon

餃子の皮

Gyoza

Harusame

RAMEN: REGIONAL SPECIALTIES

There are many kinds of ramen, and each region has its own specialty. The main differentiating factors are the specific broths and toppings, which are detailed in this tour of the most famous ramen in Japan!

全国の ラーメン

Yamagata
Cold soy sauce (sho[y]
and fish broth
Specific toppings:
cucumber, wakame

Hakata
Pork tonkotsu broth
Specific toppings: benishoga,
sesame seeds (see p. 65)

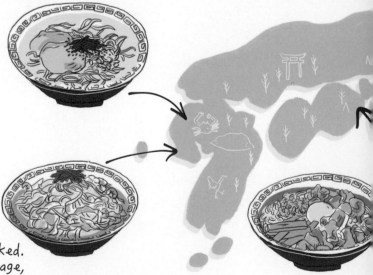

Champon Nagazaki
Thick chicken and pork broth
in which ramen noodles are cooked.
Specific toppings: seafood, cabbage,
onion, carrot

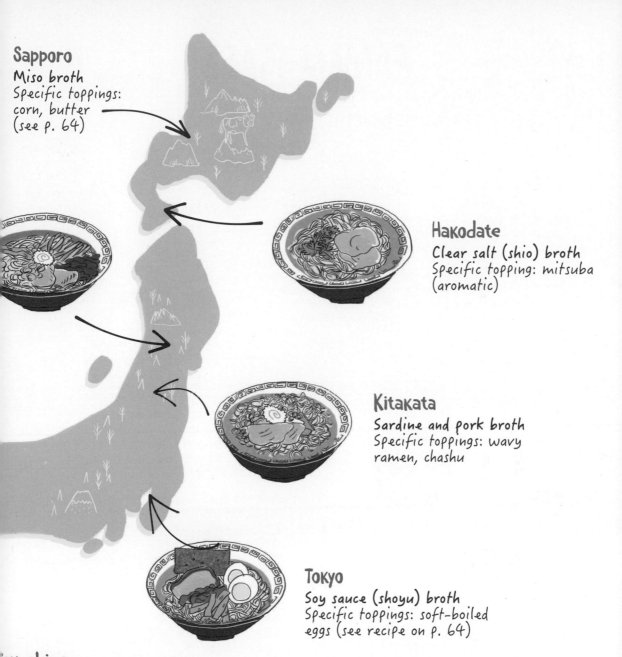

Sapporo
Miso broth
Specific toppings:
corn, butter
(see p. 64)

Hakodate
Clear salt (shio) broth
Specific topping: mitsuba
(aromatic)

Kitakata
Sardine and pork broth
Specific toppings: wavy
ramen, chashu

Tokyo
Soy sauce (shoyu) broth
Specific toppings: soft-boiled
eggs (see recipe on p. 64)

Tokushima
Pork tonkotsu and shoyu broth
Specific toppings: slices
of caramelized pork belly
(butabara), raw egg

RAMEN BASES

STEPS FOR MAKING HOMEMADE RAMEN

SERVES 4

Broth

1. Cover 2 lb. (1 kg) pork bones and 1 lb. (½ kg) chicken bones in water in a big pot, bring to a boil and cook for 5 minutes. Drain and rinse the bones.

2. In a big pot, bring the blanched bones; 1 leek; 6 crushed garlic cloves; 1½ in. (4 cm) piece of ginger, minced; 1 shallot and 1 piece of kombu seaweed to a boil in 4 qt. (4 L) chicken broth, covered. Let simmer for 2 hours.

3. Strain the broth into another pot and discard the flavorings. The broth is ready!

Chashu Meat

1. Prepare the tare sauce: Bring 3 crushed garlic cloves; ¾ in. (2 cm) piece of ginger, minced; ½ cup (125 ml) soy sauce; 2 tbsp. (30 ml) mirin; ½ cup (125 ml) sake; ½ cup (125 ml) water and 3 tbsp. (45 ml) sugar to a boil.

2. Place 1½ lb. (700 g) non-smoked pork belly or pork loin in baking dish. Drizzle the sauce overtop and bake at 275°F (130°C) for about 2 hours, turning the meat every 30 minutes.

3. Drain the meat, keeping the cooking juices. Cut into slices.

Cooking the Noodles

1. Cook 4 portions of noodles according to the package directions.

2. While the ramen noodles are cooking, prepare the serving bowl with a half-ladle of the cooking juices from the meat and 2 ladles of pork broth. Combine.

3. Drain the noodles and gently place them in the broth.

Toppings

While toppings can vary from region to region, some ingredients are consistently found in bowls of ramen.

Chashu:
slow-cooked pork
(see recipe opposite)

チャーシュー

Negi:
chopped green onion

葱心

Tamago:
soft-boiled egg

玉卵

Surimi:
Japanese fish
paste

海苔

Corn:
cooked corn
kernels

とうもろこし

Nori:
sheets of
seaweed for
a touch of
iodine

もやし

Moyashi:
Blanched soybean
sprouts

メンマ

Nenma:
lacto-fermented
bamboo shoots

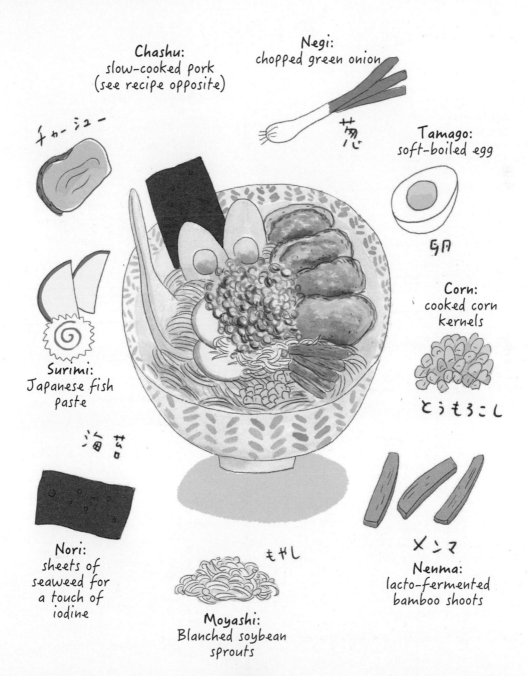

RAMEN RECIPES

MAKES ABOUT 4 BOWLS OF EACH

SHOYU RAMEN: TOKYO RAMEN

Broth: 6 cups (1.5 L) broth (see recipe on p. 62).

Soy sauce seasoning: ⅔ cup (150 ml) tare sauce (see recipe on p. 62).

Toppings: Slices of chashu (see p. 62), bamboo shoots, chopped green onion, wakame and soft-boiled eggs cut in half.

Assembly: Divide the sauce among the bowls, add the hot broth and then add the cooked and drained ramen noodles. Arrange the toppings on the noodles. Serve immediately!

醤油
らーめん

MISO RAMEN: SAPPORO RAMEN

味噌
らーめん

Broth: 6 cups (1.5 L) broth from the recipe on p. 62.

Miso seasoning: Bring 2 crushed garlic cloves; ⅓ in. (2 cm) piece of ginger, minced; ⅓ cup (75 ml) miso; 2 tbsp. (30 ml) mirin; ⅓ cup (75 ml) sake; ¼ cup (60 ml) water; 1 tbsp. (15 ml) sugar and ½ tsp. (2 ml) salt to a boil.

Toppings: Slices of chashu (see p. 62), bamboo shoots, chopped green onion, soft-boiled eggs cut in half, corn and a knob of butter.

Assembly: Combine the seasoning and broth. Divide the cooked and drained ramen noodles among the bowls. Pour in the broth, and then arrange the toppings on the noodles. Add the knob of butter last.

TONKOTSU RAMEN: HAKATA RAMEN

豚骨
らーめん

Tonkotsu broth: 6 cups (1.5 L) broth (see p. 62), adding ¾ lb. (400 g) unsalted fresh pork belly with the bones and cook for 1 hour. You will end up with a fattier and thicker broth.

Seasoning: ⅔ cup (150 ml) tare sauce (see recipe on p. 62).

Toppings: Slices of chashu (see p. 62), chopped green onion, benishoga (pickled ginger) and sesame seeds.

Assembly: Divide the sauce among the bowls, pour in the hot broth and then add the cooked and drained ramen noodles. Arrange the toppings on the noodles.

TANTAN MEN

Broth: 6 cups (1.5 L) broth (see recipe on p. 62).

Spicy seasoning: This comes entirely from the spicy pork. Cook 1 garlic clove and 2 chopped shallots in a bit of toasted sesame oil in a pan, stirring. Add ¾ lb. (400 g) ground pork and cook for 3 to 5 minutes. Add ¼ cup (60 ml) soy sauce, ¼ cup (60 ml) sesame paste, 2 tbsp. (30 ml) chili paste and ½ tsp. (2 ml) salt. Combine and cook for 1 more minute.

Toppings: Spicy pork (see recipe above) and cooked bok choy.

Assembly: Pour the boiling broth over the spicy pork. Boil for 2 minutes. Divide the cooked and drained ramen noodles among the bowls. Pour in the broth with the meat and garnish with bok choy.

担々麺

担々麺

SOBA

HOT RECIPE: KAMO NANBAN SOBA

鴨南蛮

SERVES 4

1 Cook 1 duck breast skin side down in a pan over high heat for 5 minutes. Season with salt and pepper. Flip it and continue cooking for another 2 minutes. Place it on a board and thinly slice. Remove the fat from the pan and cook 1 sliced leek for 3 to 4 minutes, stirring. Add half a glass of dashi broth, lower the heat and cook until the liquid starts to evaporate.

2 Bring ⅓ cup (75 ml) mirin and 2 tbsp. (30 ml) sake to a boil, so the alcohol cooks off, and then add 6 tbsp. (90 ml) soy sauce and 1 tbsp. (15 ml) sugar. Bring back to a boil, and then lower the heat and let the sauce reduce by half. Add the rest of the dashi broth and bring everything back to a boil.

3 Cook 12 oz. (350 g) cha soba (green tea soba) in a pot of boiling water according to the package directions (4 to 5 minutes). Drain the noodles and divide them among 4 large bowls. Add the leek and slices of duck. Add the hot broth on top.

4 Garnish with a few sprigs of mitsuba and green onion, chopped. Sprinkle with sansho powder (optional). Serve immediately.

COLD RECIPE: ZARU SOBA

ざる蕎麦

SERVES 4

1 Prepare the tsuyu sauce: Cook 1 handful of katsuobushi (dried bonito flakes), ½ cup (125 ml) soy sauce, ½ cup (125 ml) mirin, ¼ cup (60 ml) sake and 1¼ cup (300 ml) water in a saucepan on medium heat. Once boiling, turn off the heat and let the mixture cool. Strain the sauce. Refrigerate until ready to serve.

2 Meanwhile, cook 12 oz. (350 g) noodles in a pot of boiling water according to the package directions (4 to 5 minutes). Run them under cold water and drain them well. Arrange them on a serving dish with a mat. Garnish with kizami nori (shredded nori).

3 Eat the noodles by dipping them in the tsuyu sauce, seasoned with wasabi and chopped green onion.

UDON

KITSUNE UDON
SERVES 4

きつね
うどん

Aburaage
(fried tofu)

油あげ

葱
Green onion

Spinach

ほうれん草

なると
Surimi

1. Dip 2 pieces of fried tofu (aburaage) in a pot of boiling water for 1 minute to remove a bit of oil. Drain. Cut each piece of aburaage diagonally into 2 pieces and again in 2 to make triangles.

2. Place the triangles in a saucepan with 1¼ cup (300 ml) tsuyu sauce (see recipe on p. 67). Cover, bring to a boil and cook for 3 minutes. Then add 5 cups (1.2 L) dashi broth and bring back to a boil.

3. Cook 9 oz. (250 g) dried udon noodles in a pot of boiling water according to the package directions (4 to 5 minutes). Drain.

4. Divide the noodles among 4 large bowls. Pour the hot broth on top, and then place the triangles of aburaage, a few slices of surimi and steamed spinach. Garnish with chopped green onion.

NABEYAKI UDON

SERVES 2

鍋焼きうどん

1. Cook 14 oz. (400 g) thick udon noodles (fresh or frozen) in a pot of boiling water according to the package directions. Rinse them under cold water and drain well.

2. Remove the stems from 2 fresh shiitake mushrooms.

3. Combine 3 cups (750 ml) dashi broth (see recipe on p. 22), 2 tbsp. (30 ml) soy sauce, 2 tbsp. (30 ml) mirin and ½ tsp. (2 ml) salt in a saucepan.

4. Add the noodles, 1 leek sliced diagonally, the shiitake mushrooms, 3 oz. (80 g) cooked spinach, 4 slices of surimi and 4 shrimp tempura (see recipe on p. 77). Gently add 2 eggs in the center. Cover, bring to a boil and then simmer for about 5 minutes over low heat.

OTHER NOODLES

COLD SOMEN WITH EGGPLANT

SERVES 2

1 Bring 1¼ cup (300 ml) tsuyu sauce to a boil (see recipe on p. 67). Place 2 pieces of fried eggplant (recipe below) in a shallow bowl and pour the sauce on top. Let it rest until it cools to room temperature, and then refrigerate until it's time to add the dressing.

2 Cook 7 oz. (200 g) somen in a pot of boiling water according to package directions (about 2 minutes). Run under cold water and drain well.

3 Serve the noodles in 2 bowls, dividing the drained fried eggplants among the bowls and adding 1 shiso leaf, 1 chunk of grated daikon and 1 tsp. (5 ml) freshly grated ginger to each. Drizzle with tsuyu sauce and scatter chopped green onion overtop.

素麺 SoMen

揚げ茄子

FRIED EGGPLANT: AGENASU

1 Cut 1 eggplant in half lengthwise, and then cut in half again.

2 Make evenly spaced cuts into the skin of the eggplant to create a crisscross pattern.

3 Fry the pieces of eggplant for about 2 minutes. Drain.

YAKISOBA

SERVES 2

焼きそば

1 Run 10 oz. (300 g) fresh yakisoba noodles under hot water and drain well.

2 Fry 1¼ lb. (600 g) unsalted pork slices and 2 chopped onions in a bit of oil.
Add 2 chopped shiitake mushrooms, and then 4 sliced leaves of cabbage.

3 Add the noodles and cook for 1 minute, stirring. Add 1 tbsp. (15 ml) yakisoba sauce and
completely coat all the ingredients.

4 Divide the prepared mixture among the plates. Garnish with slices of red pickled ginger and
sprinkle with aonori seaweed. Serve immediately.

GYOZA

MAKES 20 GYOZA

The ingredients

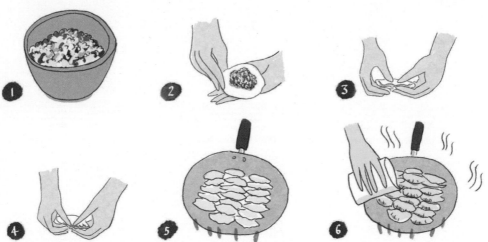

| Gyoza wrapper | Green onions | Cabbage | Ginger | Garlic | Sesame oil | Ground pork | Soy sauce | Salt & pepper |

1. Combine 4 oz. (120 g) ground pork, 4 oz. (120 g) blanched and finely sliced cabbage leaves, 1 chopped green onion, 1 minced garlic clove, 1 tsp. (5 ml) freshly grated ginger, 3 tbsp. (45 ml) soy sauce, 1 tbsp. (15 ml) sesame oil, salt and freshly ground pepper in a bowl.

2. Place a heaping teaspoon of filling in the middle of 20 gyoza wrappers.

3. Wet the edges of the top half of a wrapper. Fold it in half to close the dumpling, ensuring no air is trapped inside. Seal the edges.

4. Fold the perimeter like an accordion to firmly seal the gyoza. Repeat to shape the rest of the dumplings.

5. Heat a bit of oil in a pan, and then brown the gyoza for 3 minutes on one side.

6. Pour water halfway up the pan, cover and cook over high heat until the water has completely evaporated. Remove the lid and continue cooking for 1 minute.

7. Eat the gyoza while still hot, dipping them in a mixture of soy sauce and rice vinegar.

餃子 gyoza

家庭料理

OTHER SIGNATURE DISHES

Japanese cuisine offers a wide range of prepared foods. There are stews like nikujaga, shabu shabu and sukiyaki, fried dishes like tempura and tonkatsu, steamed dishes like chawanmushi, and much more. There are many dishes that deserve to be highlighted and demonstrate that Japanese cuisine is much more than sushi!

TEMPURA

Tempura was originally a Portuguese dish and was introduced to Japan by missionaries. These fritters, served with a mixture of dashi and soy sauce for dipping, have become a great classic of Japanese cuisine. Tempura can be used in many ways, including in donburi (on a bed of rice), in noodle soup and in bento. The most common ingredients are shrimp, fish, shiitake mushrooms, sweet potato, pumpkin and even bell peppers.

天ぷら
そば

Tempura soba

Tempura is light and crispy, thanks to its thin batter. The secret to this is the contrast between the cold batter (it's important to keep it in the fridge or to put it on ice) and the hot oil, which creates thermal shock.

Ten-don
(tempura
donburi)

天丼

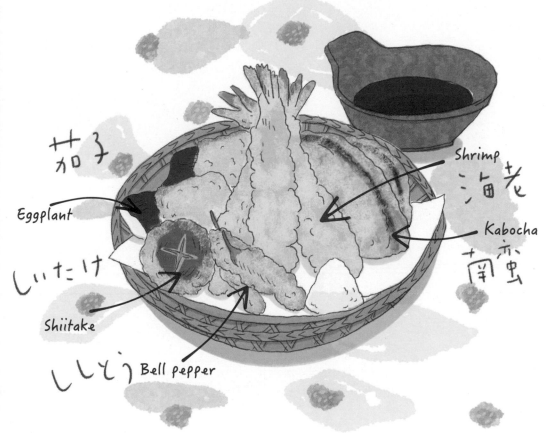

茄子
Eggplant

しいたけ
Shiitake

ししとう Bell pepper

Shrimp
海老

Kabocha
南瓜

SERVES 4

1 Peel 8 shrimp, leaving the tail, and then cut along the back and remove the black vein with the tip of the knife.

2 Combine ¾ cup (175 ml) tempura flour with ⅔ cup (150 ml) ice water in a bowl.

3 Dip the shrimp and 1 eggplant, chopped into 8 pieces; 1/4 kabocha (Japanese pumpkin), sliced; 1 deseeded green pepper chopped into 8 pieces and 4 shiitake mushrooms in the tempura batter, and then immediately immerse the prepared shrimp and vegetables in the oil. Fry until lightly colored, and then drain on paper towel. Work in batches, so as not to crowd the pot and lower the temperature of the oil.

4 Grate ¼ daikon. Arrange the tempura on a plate with a bit of grated daikon. To eat, dip the tempura in 1¼ cups (300 ml) tsuyu sauce (see recipe on p. 67), garnishing with the remaining grated daikon.

とんかつ TONKATSU

SERVES 2

1 Beat 1 egg in a shallow plate. Spread some flour and bread crumbs on two other plates. Salt and pepper 2 pork cutlets.

2 Coat with flour, then beaten egg and finally bread crumbs.

3 Fry the breaded meat in oil for about 5 minutes, until nicely golden. Drain on paper towel.

4 Thinly slice a bit of cabbage and some cucumber, and quarter 1 tomato. Divide the vegetables among the plates. Cut the meat in strips and arrange on the plates. Drizzle with tonkatsu sauce (see p. 17). Serve with a bowl of rice.

KOROKKE

MAKES 6 CROQUETTES

1. Boil 6 potatoes for about 20 minutes in a pot of salted water. Drain and peel. Mash with a fork in a big bowl.

2. Separate the whites and yolks of 2 eggs. Chop 1 onion and 1 carrot and cook in a pan with a little sunflower oil over medium heat for about 3 minutes, stirring. Add ½ lb. (200 g) salted ground beef. Cook for 4 to 5 minutes more over high heat.

3. Incorporate the mashed potatoes. Remove from the heat, add the egg yolks and combine. Season with more salt and pepper.

4. Form 6 balls from the mixture.

5. Beat the egg whites in a bowl. Put some potato starch on a plate and panko bread crumbs on another. Coat each ball with potato starch, then egg whites and lastly panko.

6. Heat oil in a wok or deep frying pan and then cook the balls for about 5 minutes, until they are nice and golden. Drain them on paper towel.

コロッケ

FISH

YAKI ZAKANA: GRILLED FISH
SERVES 2

1. Preheat oven to 400°F (200°C).

2. Place 2 sanma (or mackerel or even herring), gutted and scaled, on a baking sheet lined with parchment paper.

3. Rub a bit of salt into the skin of the fish. Bake for 15 to 20 minutes, flipping mid-way. Serve with lemon wedges, ¼ grated daikon and a bit of soy sauce.

KATSUO TATAKI: GRILLED BONITO SASHIMI

カ katsuo
魚堅のたたき
の作り方

1 Grate fresh ginger.

2 Grill the bonito fillets on a barbecue until they are golden brown on all sides (a few seconds is enough).

3 Immerse the fillets in ice water.

4 Cut the fillets into slices with a sashimi knife.

5 Arrange the bonito slices on a serving plate. Garnish with grated daikon and ginger, shiso leaves and chopped green onion. Serve with ponzu sauce (see recipe on p. 85).

ALL ABOUT SOY

Soybeans have been an essential ingredient in Japanese cuisine for millennia. This highly nutritious legume is used as the base for many products with unique flavors, particularly when the beans are fermented. Miso and soy sauce — which provide the famous umami, the fifth taste, that gives depth to dishes — are the best known and most characteristic soy-based ingredients in Japanese cuisine.

Soy Products

Momen tofu:
Firm and solid tofu. It can be cut into cubes and fried.

Kinu tofu:
Also called "silken tofu." It has a smooth and creamy consistency.

Aburaage:
Tofu cut into thin slices then fried. Used for making inari sushi and in soups.

Tonyu:
Also called soy milk, this beverage is made from soybeans and water.

Atsuage:
Thick fried tofu. Often used in stews.

Yuba:
The film left on the surface of soy milk when it is boiled.

Koyadofu:
Freeze-dried tofu. It becomes spongy. Often used in the cuisine of Zen temples.

Natto:
Fermented soybeans, which develop a strong and pronounced flavor.

Okara:
The leftover pulp of soy when it is filtered to make soy milk.

Kinako:
Roasted soy powder, which is sprinkled on desserts like daifuku or mochi.

Shoyu:
This is the famous soy sauce, essential in Japanese cooking. It is made from soybeans, wheat, water and salt.

Miso:
Fermented paste, often made from soybeans, salt, and barley or rice. It's the main ingredient in miso soup.

Homemade tofu

Homemade Tofu

1 Soak the soybeans in water overnight and then blend them with enough water to make "soy milk."

2 Bring to a boil and cook over low heat for 30 minutes.

3 Strain to separate the tonyu (milk) from the okara (soy pulp).

4 Heat the milk. Dissolve ¼ tsp. (1 ml) nigari (magnesium chloride) for every quart (or liter) of milk in a bit of water. Add the nigari mixture to the hot milk and combine. The milk will begin to curdle. Cover and let rest for 15 minutes.

5 Pour the coagulated milk into a mold lined with a thin cloth (the mold must be perforated). Cover with a cloth and place a weight on top. Let drain for about 20 minutes.

6 Remove the tofu from the mold and place in a bowl of cold water to let it cool and firm up for 15 minutes. It's ready!

SHABU SHABU

"Shabu shabu" is an onomatopoeia, said to evoke the sound that slices of beef make when held at the end of chopsticks and swished around in broth. This classic dish is the Japanese equivalent of Napa (Chinese) hot pots. The idea is to cook vegetables and slices of beef throughout the meal in a broth placed on a burner in the middle of the table.

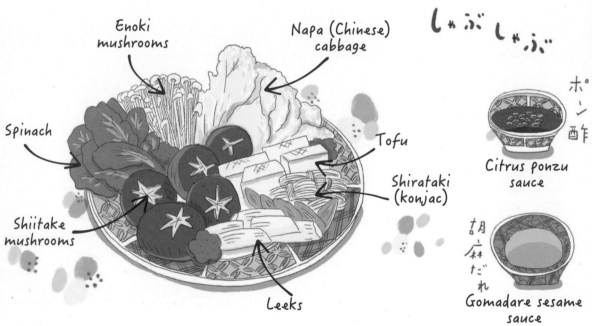

Enoki mushrooms

Napa (Chinese) cabbage

しゃぶ しゃぶ

Spinach

Tofu

Shirataki (konjac)

ポン酢

Citrus ponzu sauce

Shiitake mushrooms

胡麻だれ

Gomadare sesame sauce

Leeks

Broth

Let a piece of kombu seaweed infuse in a pot filled with water for 30 minutes. Bring the mixture to a simmer, and remove the kombu before the mixture begins to boil.

Meat

In Japan, shabu shabu can be a refined dish when it is made with Wagyu beef, which is a very luxurious type of Japanese beef that has perfect marbling and melts in your mouth. Sirloin is also an excellent option. It is very important to cut very thin slices of meat (you can freeze the meat beforehand to make slicing easier) and to cook the slices for only a short time in the broth (a few seconds may suffice). You can also use pork, in which case you will likely want to cook a bit longer.

Sauces

Shabu shabu can be served with two different sauces: gomadare sesame sauce (see recipe p. 25) and citrus ponzu sauce (see recipe opposite).

しゃぶ しゃぶ

When you're ready to eat, dip the vegetables one at a time into the broth. Enjoy shabu shabu by poaching the slices of meat and tofu in the broth before dipping them in a small bowl of gomadare or ponzu sauce.

INGREDIENTS FOR ABOUT 1 CUP (250 ML) OF PONZU SAUCE (PREPARE THE DAY BEFORE)

1 Combine 1 small handful of dried bonito (or 1 dried shiitake, sold in Asian grocery stores), 2 in. (5 cm) dried kombu seaweed, ⅔ cup (150 ml) soy sauce, ⅓ cup (75 ml) lemon juice, ¼ cup (60 ml) mandarin juice, ¼ cup (60 ml) mirin (sweet cooking sake) in a jar.

2 Close and let infuse in the fridge overnight. Strain the sauce the next day.

すき焼き SUKIYAKI & ODEN

Sukiyaki

This traditional dish, much like shabu shabu (see p. 84), consists of vegetables and thin slices of beef cooked throughout the meal in a pot placed on a burner in the middle of the table. But instead of being cooked in a broth, they are simmered in a sweet and salty sauce (see recipe below). The distinguishing feature of this dish is dipping the vegetables and meat in a beaten raw egg right before eating.

Sukiyaki Sauce

1 Bring ⅓ cup (75 ml) soy sauce, ⅓ cup (75 ml) mirin, ¼ cup (60 ml) sake, ¼ cup (60 ml) water and ¼ cup (60 ml) granulated sugar to a boil in a small saucepan, stirring to fully dissolve the sugar. Remove from the heat.

2 Add a little oil to the pot, and then simmer the vegetables and meat with a bit of sukiyaki sauce.

3 Serve the sukiyaki with 1 egg per person, each in a separate bowl; each person will break and lightly beat their egg before dipping the vegetables and meat as they eat.

4 Serve with a bowl of white rice.

ODEN: A JAPANESE STEW

SERVES 4

おでん

Helpful Hint
Since it can be difficult to find fish cakes or mochi in North America, you can make this recipe with other ingredients, including dumplings, potatoes or carrots.

1 Prepare the fried tofu pouches: Cut 2 aburaage (fried tofu pouches) in half. Immerse them in a pot of boiling water for a few seconds to remove excess oil. Drain on paper towel. Cut 2 mochi (sticky rice cakes) in half. Place 1 piece of mochi in each pouch. Close with toothpicks or cooked spinach stems.

2 Bring 5 cups (1.2 L) dashi broth, 2 tbsp. (30 ml) sake, 2 tbsp. (30 ml) mirin and 6 tbsp. (90 ml) soy sauce to a boil in a pot.

3 Slice ½ daikon into thick rounds. Add them to the pot along with 6 oz. (160 g) konnyaku (konjac), 7 oz. (200 g) cubed firm tofu cut and 4 hard-boiled eggs. Simmer for about 5 minutes over low heat. Add 4 chikuwa (a kind of surimi) cut in half, 4 gobo maki (fish cakes made from fish and burdock) and the fried tofu pouches. Cover and simmer for 40 minutes. A few minutes before it's finished cooking, add 1 handful of cooked spinach.

4 Place the pot on the table. Each person serves themselves based on their own tastes, taking a bit of broth and adding a dab of karashi mustard.

海藻 ALL ABOUT SEAWEED

The Japanese are the world's largest consumers of seaweed. Rich in minerals, vitamins and proteins, it is mainly found in dried forms:

Nori (のり):
This is the most-consumed seaweed and is used to make sushi rolls. It is sold in sheet form and eaten as is, with care not to get it wet.

Agar agar (寒天):
This natural gelling agent is made from red algae. It is also healthier than gelatin. To bring out its gelling qualities, it needs to be boiled for a few seconds.

Wakame (わかめ):
A key ingredient in miso soup and most salads. Sold dried, this seaweed must be rehydrated before eating.

Kombu (昆布):
This seaweed is the base for most broths and sauces in Japanese cooking. It is found mainly dried and in sheet form. It is infused in water to make the famous dashi (see p. 22).

Hijiki (ひじき):
This small seaweed is sold dried and needs to be rehydrated and cooked before eating. In Japan, it is mainly simmered with other vegetables.

Mekabu (メカブ):
This seaweed comes from the same plant as wakame. It is the central stem, close to the roots, while wakame is the leafy part. It is usually sold fresh, already cut and seasoned. It goes well with white rice.

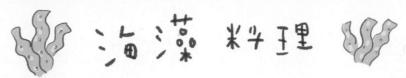

海藻 料理

SUNOMONO SALAD WITH WAKAME

1 Combine slices of cucumber with salt.

2 Rehydrate the wakame in a bowl of cold water.

3 Prepare a vinaigrette of rice vinegar, soy sauce, sugar and salt.

4 Squeeze the cucumber slices with your hands to remove the liquid.

5 Combine all of the ingredients and enjoy!

わかめ と きゅうり の 酢 の 物

昆布 の 佃煮

TSUKUDANI: A SEAWEED CONDIMENT

1 Rehydrate 5 oz. (150 g) kombu and slice into strips. Combine with ¼ cup (60 ml) water, 3 tbsp. (45 ml) soy sauce, 1 tbsp. (15 ml) mirin, 1 tbsp. (15 ml) sake, 1 tbsp. (15 ml) sugar, ½ tbsp. (7 ml) rice vinegar and 1 tsp. (5 ml) toasted sesame oil in a saucepan.

2 Bring to a boil, cover and let simmer over low heat until there is no more liquid.

3 Once cooked, add sesame seeds.

4 Tsukudani keeps for several weeks in the refrigerator and can be eaten on white rice.

鉄板焼き TEPPANYAKI

Teppanyaki ("teppan" means "stainless iron") is a method of quickly cooking food on an iron plate. In Japan, there are many teppanyaki restaurants where the chef cooks in front of customers, who are seated at a counter surrounding the grill. This type of restaurant has also taken off outside of Japan, and the concept has somewhat evolved. Chefs put on a show right before your eyes — a real ballet of spatulas and knives!

Teppanyaki Ingredients

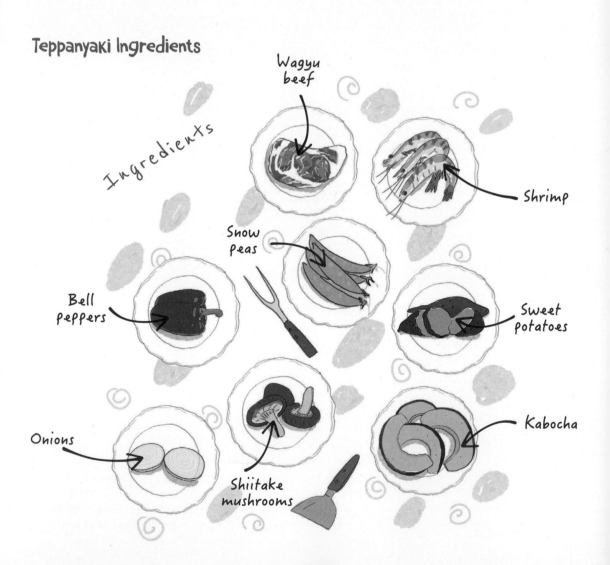

Ingredients

Wagyu beef

Shrimp

Snow peas

Bell peppers

Sweet potatoes

Onions

Shiitake mushrooms

Kabocha

ソース 胡麻 →

Yakiniku Sauce

Cook ¼ grated onion in a saucepan over high heat. When the water from the onion starts to boil, add 3 tbsp. (45 ml) soy sauce, 3 tbsp. (45 ml) mirin, 2 tbsp. (30 ml) sake and 1½ tbsp. (22 ml) granulated sugar. Boil for 1 minute. Remove from the heat and add 1 grated garlic clove and 1 tbsp. (15 ml) sesame seeds.

→ 葱 & 唐辛子

Spicy Sauce

Cook 1 tbsp. (15 ml) chili paste; ¾ in. (2 cm) ginger, grated; 1 grated garlic clove; 3 tbsp. (45 ml) soy sauce; 2 tbsp. (30 ml) mirin; ½ tbsp. (7 ml) sesame oil and 2 tbsp. (30 ml) granulated sugar for 1 minute over high heat. Remove from the heat and add 1 chopped green onion.

季節の伝統料理

CUISINE BY THEME

Life in Japan is marked by the seasons and traditional holidays, which strongly influence the cuisine. Bento are eaten under blooming cherry trees in spring, cold soba is enjoyed during the humid heat of summer, grilled matsutake (highly prized mushrooms) are eaten as soon as the maples turn red in the fall and nabe (Japanese stew) is prepared during the winter after a hot bath in natural springs. However, street food is available year round, with its ubiquitous dishes that can also be found in the friendly atmosphere of an izakaya.

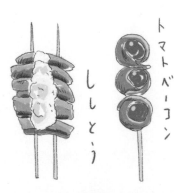

ト
マ
ト
ベ
ー
コ
ン

し
し
と
う

STREET FOOD & YAKITORI

Japan, known for its refined cuisine, also offers amazing street food. Whether during matsuri (festivals) or particular neighborhoods of big cities (notably Fukuoka on the island of Kyushu), rows of food stalls, called "yatai," offer various popular dishes, including takoyaki (p. 97), yakisoba (p. 71), ramen (p. 60) and the famous yakitori (see opposite).

Yakitori yatai

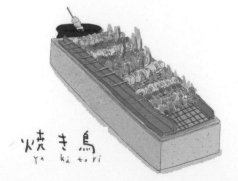

焼き鳥
Ya ki to ri

Yakitori

Yakitori (literally "grilled chicken") is a real Japanese institution. They are small savory skewers cooked on a barbecue and normally dipped in a sauce called "yakitori sauce." Yakitori is traditionally made with chicken, but there are many varieties available, featuring vegetables and other meats.

YAKITORI
焼き鳥

つくね

Tsukune:
ground chicken
balls

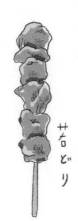
若どり

**Chicken
thigh**

ささみ梅しそ

**Sasami ume
shiso:** chicken
breast with
umeboshi and
shiso

きも

Kimo:
chicken
liver

アスパラベーコン

Aspara-bacon:
asparagus
wrapped in
bacon

白ねぎ

Shiro negi:
leeks

しいたけ

Shiitake:
mushrooms

ししとう

Shishitou:
bell peppers
and grated
daikon

トマトベーコン

Tomato-bacon:
tomatoes
wrapped in
bacon

皮

Kawa:
chicken
skin

ねぎま

Neguima:
chicken and
green onion

手羽先

Tebasaki:
chicken
wings

お好み焼き OKONOMIYAKI
Okonomiyaki

MAKES 1 LARGE PANCAKE

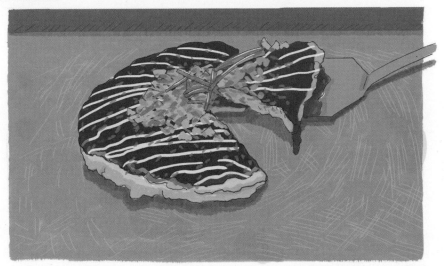

小麦粉

Flour

たまご

Eggs

せんぎり キャベツ

Cabbage

薄切り豚肉

Pork belly

マヨネーズ

Mayonnaise

1 Slice 4 thin slices of pork belly into strips. Fry them for 3 minutes over medium heat in a pan without any oil.

2 Combine 1 cup (250 ml) white flour, 1 egg and ½ cup (125 ml) dashi broth (see p. 22) in a bowl. Add the pork belly, 1 cup (250 ml) shredded cabbage and 1 chopped green onion.

3 Pour the mixture onto an oiled griddle (or frying pan), spreading it out like a pancake with a spatula. Cook for 3 minutes over high heat, and then flip the pancake and cook for 5 minutes longer on medium heat.

4 Flip again and cook for another 5 minutes. Flip the pancake for the final time and cook for another 3 minutes.

5 Serve the pancake brushed with a little okonomiyaki sauce (see p. 17) and Japanese mayonnaise. If desired, garnish with katsuobushi (dried bonito flakes), benishoga (pickled ginger) and aonori seaweed flakes.

TAKOYAKI

Takoyaki, literally "grilled octopus," are small grilled dough balls stuffed with octopus and topped with mayonnaise and takoyako sauce, which is sweet and salty (and very similar to okonomiyaki sauce). This speciality of Osaka has become the symbol of Japanese street food. Here is the recipe, so you can make them at home — however, a takoyaki grill is essential!!

た こ 焼 き
ta ko ya ki

1 Combine ¾ cup (175 ml) flour, 1 egg, 1¼ cup (300 ml) dashi broth (see p. 22), 1 tbsp. (15 ml) milk, ½ tbsp. (7 ml) soy sauce and 1 pinch of salt in a bowl.

2 Heat and oil the takoyaki grill. Drop batter in the holes, and then divide the filling — diced cooked octopus, benishoga (pickled ginger), tenkasu (tempura flakes) and chopped green onion — in the center of each portion of batter. When halfway cooked (about 2 minutes), flip each ball with a metal pick (it takes a bit of practice!). Eat the balls topped with takoyaki sauce, Kewpie mayonnaise and aonori seaweed flakes.

居酒屋 IZAKAYA

With their lantern and noren (curtains) at their entrance, izakaya have become indispensable in Japan, offering a unique experience — a true immersion into Japanese culture. Literally a "place to drink alcohol," izakaya are a popular type of restaurant. It's a convivial place where you share dishes among friends or colleagues, generally over a glass of beer or sake. A meal at an izakaya consists of a multitude of small dishes, ranging from the most traditional to the most creative, where each person picks their portion from a small plate. These are real Japanese tapas, where the delicacy of the flavors is shared in a friendly atmosphere.

Izakaya are mainly for grazing and drinking, as different dishes are tasted and shared. This allows you to mix things up. You can have your favorite dishes but also discover new flavors!

Kanpai! In Japan, you cheers by saying "kanpai" — and not cin cin, which would make the Japanese laugh because it means "penis"!

Oshibori: When you arrive at an izakaya, start by ordering a drink, which will arrive with an oshibori, a wonderful hot, wet towel that you use to clean your hands (it's not recommended for your face) and will perk you up after a long day!

かんぱい

TOP 10 IZAKAYA DISHES
居酒屋

NO. 1: AGEDASHI TOFU 揚げ出し豆腐
SERVES 4

1. Prepare the sauce: Combine ⅔ cup (150 ml) dashi broth (see p. 22), 3 tbsp. (45 ml) soy sauce, 2 tbsp. (30 ml) mirin and 1 pinch of salt in a saucepan. Reduce for about 10 minutes over low heat.

2. Slice 14 oz. (400 g) silken tofu (drained in advance for 2 hours) into 4 pieces and coat in potato starch.

3. Heat oil in a wok or deep frying pan, and then fry the tofu pieces until they take on a nice golden color. Drain on paper towel.

4. Place the fried tofu in a serving bowl. Pour the sauce on top and garnish with grated daikon and ginger, katsuobushi (dried bonito flakes) and chopped green onion. Sprinkle with shichimi togarashi (Japanese 7 spice blend).

Tamagoyaki:
Japanese omelet
(see recipe on p. 52)

Korokke:
potato croquettes
(see recipe on p. 79)

Edamame:
young soybeans cooked in
water and salted

Yakitori: chicken or
vegetable skewers (see
recipe on p. 95)

Karaage: marinated
fried chicken

Tebasaki: fried
chicken wings

Potato salad: potato and
cucumber salad with
mayonnaise

Onigiri: rice balls
(see recipe on p. 47)

Hiyayakko: kinu tofu
(silken tofu) served cold
and seasoned
(see p. 107)

NEW YEAR: OSECHI RYORI

Osechi ryori is the new year meal. Dishes are prepared in advance and presented in a traditional layered bento called a "jubako." Each dish and ingredient has a specific meaning, creating a strongly symbolic meal.

御節 料理

Kazunoko: herring roe, which symbolizes a growing family

Kamaboko: fish cakes, which evoke the first sunrise of the year

Kombu maki: kombu seaweed rolls, for joy

Kuromame: black beans, for good health

Tazukuri: sweet and salty sardines, which symboliz the hope for a good harvest

Renkon: lotus root, for an unfettered future

Ebi: shrimp, for longevity

Date maki: sweet omelet, for a good future

お雑煮

Ozoni

This soup celebrates the beginning of the new year. Made from a dashi broth base, it contains vegetables and sometimes meat and mochi. This sticky rice cake is mainly eaten during the new year period, and its shape, like its cooking method, varies depending on the region.

お酒

Ootoso Sake

The first sake of the year is consumed before the osechi to purify oneself after the previous year and to inspire good health in the new year. There is a ritual for drinking this medicinal sake: Each family member (from youngest to oldest) takes a drink from each of the three cups, starting with the smallest.

年越しそば

Toshikoshi Soba

"Toshikoshi" literally means "crossing over from one year to the next." This simple soba noodle broth (see recipe on p. 66) is eaten on new year's eve. This tradition is largely followed in Japan, as it allows you to cross over into the new year feeling light, having eaten a dish of noodles simply garnished with chopped green onion and a kamaboko (fish cake).

春 SPRING

Spring in Japan is closely tied to sakura (cherry trees). Their ephemeral blossoms are celebrated by all Japanese people during hanami, which literally means "the contemplation of flowers." Most often, it means picnicking under a cherry tree in bloom with friends, family or even coworkers.

お花見

Sake

Sakura mochi

Spring bento

During hanami, you eat bento (see p. 50) and drink (a lot!) of beer or sake. The typical sweet snack of this time of year is sakura mochi. This mochi (see p. 118), filled with anko paste (see p. 116), is colored light pink to evoke the cherry blossoms and wrapped in a pickled cherry leaf — a real delight!

Prepare Fresh Bamboo Shoots

Peel and cook them in plenty of water (ideally the water used to rinse rice, which is rich in starch) for at least an hour and a half. Drain, after which they are ready to be eaten or prepared.

"Shun" is an important concept in Japanese cuisine, especially in spring, because it refers to the exact moment when a vegetable is at its peak. This is the case for bamboo shoots (takenoko), which start poking through in early May and which must be dug up at the exact moment when the tips lift the earth.

竹
旬のたきこみ
ごはん

Takenoko Gohan

In this dish, which literally means "bamboo rice," prepared bamboo shoots are cooked directly with rice in dashi broth seasoned with soy sauce, mirin and sake.

竹
旬の煮物

Simmered Takenoko

Chop 1 large bamboo shoot into 8 pieces. Place ⅓ cup (75 ml) dried bonito in a tea filter. Arrange the bamboo pieces and dried bonito in a saucepan. Add 2½ cups (625 ml) dashi broth (see p. 22), ¼ cup (60 ml) soy sauce and ¼ cup (60 ml) mirin. Bring to a boil and cook over low heat for 30 minutes. Let cool in the sauce, and eat at room temperature.

夏 SUMMER

Summer is a very festive season, with many matsuri (festivals) and hanabi (fireworks). Matsuri are popular festivals that take place throughout Japan. Festivalgoers in yukata (summer kimonos) attend for fun, enjoying the wide array of treats offered by the many food stalls. Since summer in Japan is synonymous with heat and humidity, fresh dishes are always appreciated at this time of year.

祭リ

かき氷

Kakigori

This shaved ice drenched in brightly colored syrup is a matsuri must. Unlike a simple granita, kakigori is made with a machine that finely shaves a block of ice. The result is airy, with a texture similar to snow!

Hiya Yakko (Fresh Tofu)

Drain a block of silken tofu (kinu tofu). Slice into 4 pieces and place in a small dish. Garnish with chopped green onion, grated ginger and katsuobushi (dried bonito flakes). Drizzle with ponzu sauce (see p. 85) or a little soy sauce.

冷やっこ

土糸麦面

Hiyashi Somen (Cold Noodles)

Cook somen noodles in boiling water according to package directions. Rinse the noodles in cold water and place them in a shallow bowl with ice cubes. Eat them by dipping them in a tsuyu sauce (see p. 67) with yakumi (grated ginger, chopped myoga and chopped green onion).

FALL

In the fall, Japan is blanketed in the colors of momiji (maple trees): red and yellow. Koyo ("red leaf" as well as "fall leaf viewing") and momijigari (literally "maple hunting") are fall's equivalent of spring's hanami: the contemplation of autumnal colors at the peak of the season. These autumnal colors are also found in dishes that feature persimmons, kabocha, mushrooms and even sweet snacks in the shape of maple leaves!

Persimmons

Permissions are Japan's national fruit. With the arrival of fall, persimmon trees brimming with these orange-colored fruits can be found throughout the countryside. There is a wide range of persimmon varieties, but the persimmons in Japan are rarely acidic, meaning they don't need to be frozen before eating, as is common in other parts of the world. Persimmons are also dried in order to be eaten throughout the year, such as hoshigaki (dried persimmon), which are a sweet snack often served with tea.

松茸
Grilled Matsutake

Mushroom lovers are delighted with Japanese cuisine, which offers a wonderful array of mushroom varieties. They are all equally tasty: shimeji, shiitake, enoki, nameko and matsutake, the king of mushrooms. Literally "pine mushroom," matsuke grow in pine forests. Their rarity and delicate flesh make them an expensive and refined food. They can be cooked with rice, tempura style, teppanyaki style, in broth or simply grilled with a little sudachi (a Japanese citrus fruit).

かぼちゃ
Kabocha

This Japanese squash with green skin has a tender texture and a flavor similar to chestnut; it can be used in salty or sweet dishes. Kabocha can be used in salads, stews and tempura. It is most often stewed, as in kabocha soboro, in which cubes of kabocha are simmered with ground chicken in a dashi broth seasoned with soy sauce, mirin, sake and sugar. When the kabocha softens, the final step is to thicken the broth with a little potato starch diluted in water.

もみじ饅頭
Momiji Manju

Manju is a very popular dessert in Japan. As with most Japanese sweets, manju are filled with red bean paste (anko, see recipe on p. 116). Unlike mochi, which is made from sticky rice, manju is made from wheat flour. Momiji manju, which is shaped like a maple leaf, is a must-try specialty of Miyajima, an island off Hiroshima.

冬 WINTER

Japanese winters can be particularly harsh, especially in the north, in the Tohoku region and on the island of Hokkaido, where snow is abundant. To warm up, it's good to relax in an onsen, which are volcanic hot springs found throughout the archipelago. Lounging in a rotenburo (open-air bath) while admiring the surrounding snow-covered landscape is a unique experience!

温泉

Onsen Tamago

These eggs traditionally cooked in hot springs (onsen) are mainly served for breakfast. The low-temperature cooking method — around 160°F (70°C) — provides a unique texture to the egg white, which remains silky and soft, while the yolk is runny.

石焼き芋
Roasted Sweet Potato

Japanese sweet potatoes, called satsumaimo, are tender, almost sticky and very sweet. You can still find street vendors that cry "yakiimo" (roasted potatoes) to attract customers. Hot roasted sweet potatoes with skin are sold wrapped in newspaper.

蟹鍋
Kani Nabe

During the colder months, you can warm up with nabe, which are Japanese stews, such as shabu shabu (see p. 84), nabeyaki (see p. 69) and oden (see p. 87). Each region has its specialty, and kani nabe, Hokkaido's stew with king crab, is the signature nabe of the winter season. The region's famous crab is cooked in a dashi broth along with seasonal vegetables. It is recommended to finish the broth by adding cooked rice and beaten eggs, which rounds out the rich flavors of the crab and vegetables. It's an absolute marvel!

和菓子 と 飲み物

DESSERTS AND BEVERAGES

Traditional Japanese desserts called wagashi (和菓子) reflect the Japanese aesthetic, like jewels in a case, while remaining close to nature. In fact, they often follow the changing of the seasons and strongly evoke Japanese flowers through their colors, textures and shapes. To appreciate the subtleties of these sweets, it is recommended to pair them with green tea and more specifically matcha, the tea powder used for traditional tea ceremonies.

和菓子 WAGASHI

Traditional Japanese desserts are called wagashi ("wa" and "Japanese" and "kashi" and "sweet"). These small and very beautiful treats are first appreciated for their appearance and then for their refined and delicate flavor.

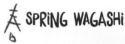 SPRING WAGASHI

Sakura nerikiri

Shibori nerikiri

Sakura manju

SUMMER WAGASHI

Kingyo kanten

Natsu shibori

Uchiwa

FALL WAGASHI

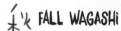

Kuri yokan

Momiji

Botan nerikiri

WINTER WAGASHI

Fuyu no happa

Fuyu nerikiri

Usagi manju

FUYU NERIKIRI

MAKES 6 TO 8 WAGASHI

1 Combine 1½ tbsp. (22 ml) sticky rice flour, 1 tbsp. (15 ml) confectioner's sugar and 1 tbsp. (15 ml) water in a bowl.

2 Add 9 oz. (250 g) shiroan (see p. 116, replacing the adzuki beans with white beans), combine and then dry the paste in a saucepan, mixing until it is no longer sticky.

3 Separate the paste into 2 portions. Add a few drops of purple food coloring to one half of the paste. Mix to obtain an even color.

4 Add green food coloring to the other half to obtain the green nerikiri.

5 Run the green nerikiri through a sieve to make small spaghettilike strands from the paste. Do the same with the purple nerikiri.

6 Take another 4 to 6 oz. (120 to 160 g) of shiroan and form 6 to 8 balls. Gently place the green and purple nerikiri spaghetti on each ball of shiroan.

DORAYAKI

MAKING ANKO (ADZUKI BEAN PASTE)

1 Soak 17 oz. (500 g) adzuki beans in plenty of cold water for at least 12 hours.

2 Drain, rinse and put the beans in a pot. Cover with water. Bring to a boil and then drain.

3 Place the beans back in the pot and cover with at least twice their volume of water. Bring back to a boil and continue cooking for 1.5 to 2 hours, making sure to add more water if needed.

4 The beans are fully cooked when they can easily be crushed between your fingers. Drain once fully cooked.

5 Run the beans through a rigid sieve (or vegetable mill), working in batches as needed.

6 Place the paste in a thick-bottomed saucepan. Add 1⅔ cups (400 ml) sugar and cook, stirring constantly, for about 10 minutes — you will end up with a smooth purée.

DORAYAKI ドラ焼き
MAKES 6 DORAYAKI

1 Beat 2 eggs, ⅓ cup (75 ml) sugar, 1 tbsp. (15 ml) honey and 1 pinch of salt together in a bowl.

2 Dilute 1 tsp. (5 ml) yeast in 1 tbsp. (15 ml) water, and then add to the bowl. Whisk, incorporating 1¼ cups (300 ml) sifted flour.

3 Heat a little oil in a pan and cook the dough in batches to get golden pancakes.

4 Spread a little anko paste on a pancake. Cover it with a second pancake. Press lightly.

5 Continue until all the dough is used.

6 Eat while still warm or store in plastic wrap.

DAIFUKU

Daifuku is one of the most popular sweet snacks in Japanese cuisine. It has sticky rice (mochi) on the outside and red bean paste (anko, see p. 116) on the inside. It's a treat that's very easy to make at home.

MAKES 8 DAIFUKU

1 Divide 7 oz. (200 g) anko paste into 8 portions and form 8 balls. Keep them in the refrigerator.

2 Combine 1 cup (250 ml) sticky rice flour, ¼ cup (60 ml) sugar and ½ cup (125 ml) water in a bowl.

3 Prepare a pot to steam the dough balls. Place the bowl of dough in the steam basket, cover and cook for 15 minutes.

4 Sift cornstarch on a work surface and place the cooked dough on top, using a silicone spatula. Coat with cornstarch (because it is very sticky); don't hesitate to use a generous amount of cornstarch! Cut the dough into 8 pieces.

5 Take one piece of dough and spread it out in the palm of your hand.

6 Place 1 scoop of anko paste onto the dough and cover it with dough. Seal the daifuku. Repeat to form the other 7 daifuku.

DIFFERENT VARIETIES

大福もち

Daifuku with Anko

This is the most classic variety (see recipe opposite).

抹茶
大福

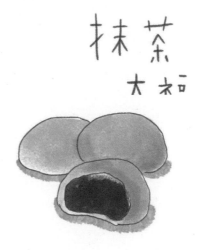

Macha Mochi

Incorporate ½ tsp. (2 ml) matcha in the mochi paste.

もち大福

Mochi Cream

Replace the ball of anko with a ball of ice cream (matcha, strawberry, black sesame, etc.).

いちご大福

Strawberry Daifuku

A whole strawberry is placed inside the white anko ball (shiroan).

BEVERAGES

自動販売機

Japanese people mainly drink tea, but sodas and energy drinks with unexpected flavors can also be found in the many vending machines on every street corner. Beer and sake (see p. 124) are the most popular alcoholic beverages.

Vending Machines

JAPANESE TEAS

  玉露

Gyokuro

This tea's name means "dew drop," and it is generally of very high quality.

    抹茶

Matcha

This tea powder is used for the famous tea ceremony.

   煎茶

Sencha

This tea represents two-thirds of Japan's production.

  玄米茶

Genmaicha

A tea blended with puffed brown rice grains.

  ほうじ茶

Hojicha

The leaves are roasted at 400°F (200°C) and then cooled. This gives them a brown appearance.

   くき茶

Kukicha

The stems and twigs of tea are also used and sometimes mixed with a small amount of leaves.

DIFFERENT TYPES OF BEVERAGES

抹茶ラテ

Matcha latte:
green tea with
steamed milk

むぎ茶

Mugicha:
a roasted barley
infusion

カルピス
ウオーター

Calpis:
a milk
beverage

ラムネ

Ramune:
Japanese lemonade

冷たい緑茶

Cold green tea

ビール

Beer:
the most widely
consumed alcoholic
beverage in Japan

柚子酒

Yuzushu:
alcohol made from
yuzus (a citrus
fruit)

酒

Sake:
rice wine
(see p. 124)

ウィスキー

Whisky:
Japan produces
high-quality
whiskies

焼酎

Shochu:
alcohol made from rice,
barley or sweet potatos

梅酒

Umeshu:
alcohol made from
umeboshi plums

茶道 THE TEA CEREMONY

The Japanese tea ceremony is a traditional art. It was Sen Rikyu who, in the 16th century, transformed the tea ceremony into a true art called "chado." The ceremony generally takes place in a specific tatami room; the guests (maximum 5) are seated in seiza (kneeling on their heels). The ceremony can last several hours, often in silence. It is a form of meditation and sharing that expresses 4 principles:

Wa (harmony)   Sei (purity)
Kei (respect)   Jaku (tranquility)

Steps of the Tea Ceremony

1. The tea powder is transferred from the box (natsume) to the bowl (chawan) with a special spoon (chashaku).

2. Hot water from the pot (kama) is poured into the bowl using a long bamboo ladle (hishaku).

3. The tea powder and water are mixed using a small bamboo whisk (chasen), which facilitates fast and precise movements.

4. The tea is ready when it has a beautiful green texture and a little foam. The bowl is then presented to the guest of honor.

5. The guest of honor receives the bowl with their right hand and places it in the palm of their left hand.

6. They turn the bowl in their left hand, using their right hand, 2 or 3 times in a clockwise direction.

7. They then drink it in two and a half sips, finishing to the last drop before placing the bowl in front of them. Only one guest drinks at a time.

酒 SAKE

Sake, called "nihonshu," is Japan's national drink. It can be defined as a rice wine and is the result of fermenting rice. Sake is a subtle drink, with an alcohol content between 14% and 17%, which is a little higher than wine.

Sake is mainly consumed cold (to best appreciate its subtle aromas), but it can also be heated to about 100°F (40°C) (particularly in winter).

Hot sake   Cold sake

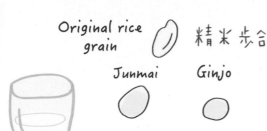

Original rice grain 精米歩合

Junmai	Ginjo	Daiginjo
70%	60%	50%
純米	吟醸	大吟醸

Rice Polishing

The rice used for sake is different from the rice used for cooking. The grains are polished to remove the husk. The more the rice is polished, the higher the quality of the sake.

Junmai sake is made from rice polished to 70%, ginjo is made from rice polished to 60% and daiginjo is more from rice polished to 50%.

Production Steps

There are four key elements that determine the quality of sake: rice, polishing, water and brewing.

1 Rice is polished (see above) and then washed.

2 The rice is steam cooked.

3 Kojikin (a type of mold) is added to a small part of the cooked rice, which becomes koji after 2 days of fermentation.

4 The koji is mixed with cooked rice along with water, which becomes shubo after an initial fermentation of 2 weeks to 1 month.

5 The shubo is combined with more koji, water and more cooked rice to make moromi, which is the main fermentation and takes around 1 month.

6 The moromi is then pressed.

7 The sake is pasteurized.

8 The sake is bottled.

RECIPE INDEX

ACKNOWLEDGEMENTS

Thank you to Aurélie for giving me the opportunity to work on projects that are dear to my heart.
It is often through encounters that projects are made possible. This book is the result of a beautiful encounter with Haruna, whose wonderful illustrations make this book a work that I am truly proud of.

I hope you enjoy it as much as I do!

Laure Kié was born in Tokyo to a Japanese mother and a French father. Her many trips to Japan allowed her to learn about the richness of Japanese culinary culture, which she passes on through her cookbooks and cooking classes.

Haruna Kishi is a Japanese writer, director and illustrator. She also writes and directs animated series, including Miru Miru.

A FIREFLY BOOK

Published by Firefly Books Ltd. 2021
First published in French by Mango, Paris, France — 2019
© Mango, Paris, 2019

2nd printing, 2022

Library of Congress Control Number: 2021933831

Library and Archives Canada Cataloguing in Publication
Title: Japanese cuisine : an illustrated guide / written by Laura Kié ; illustrated by Haruna Kishi.
Other titles: Cuisine japonaise illustrée. English
Names: Kié, Laure, author. | Kishi, Haruna, illustrator.
Description: Translation of: La cuisine japonaise illustrée. | Includes index.
Identifiers: Canadiana 2021015053X | ISBN 9780228103196 (softcover)
Subjects: LCSH: Cooking, Japanese. | LCSH: Cooking, Japanese—Pictorial works. | LCGFT: Cookbooks.
Classification: LCC TX724.5 .K5413 2021 | DDC 641.5952—dc23

Published in Canada by
Firefly Books Ltd.
50 Staples Avenue, Unit 1
Richmond Hill, Ontario
L4B 0A7

Published in the United States by
Firefly Books (U.S.) Inc.
P.O. Box 1338, Ellicott Station
Buffalo, New York
14205

Layout: Amélie Garcin
Translator: Adriana Paradiso

Printed in China

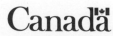 *We acknowledge the financial support of the Government of Canada.*